INSIGHT

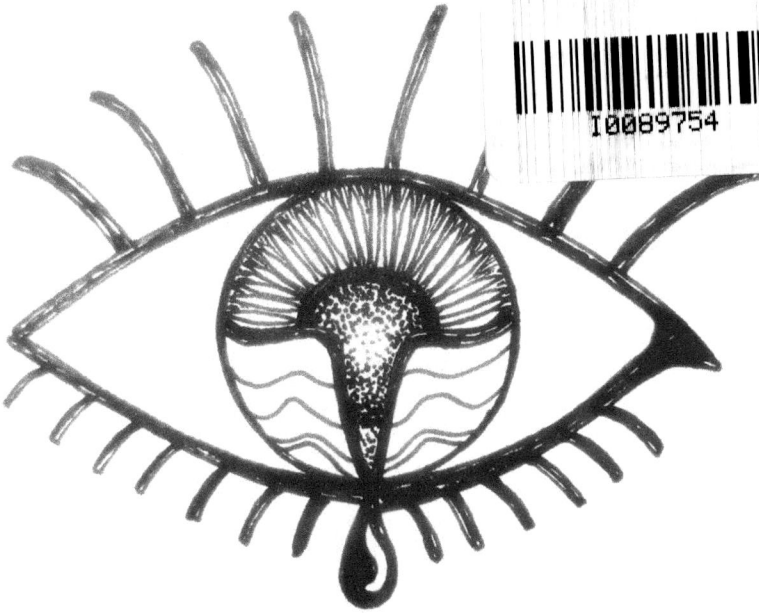

UP CLOSE AND PERSONAL
PROFILE OF SEXUAL ASSAULT

MICHELLE SLEIGHT

First published by Ultimate World Publishing 2020
Copyright © 2020 Michelle Sleight

ISBN

Paperback - 978-1-925884-96-8
Ebook - 978-1-925884-97-5

Cover design: Ultimate World Publishing
Layout and typesetting: Ultimate World Publishing
Editor: Anita Saunders

Ultimate World Publishing
Diamond Creek,
Victoria Australia 3089
www.writeabook.com.au

ULTIMATE WORLD
PUBLISHING

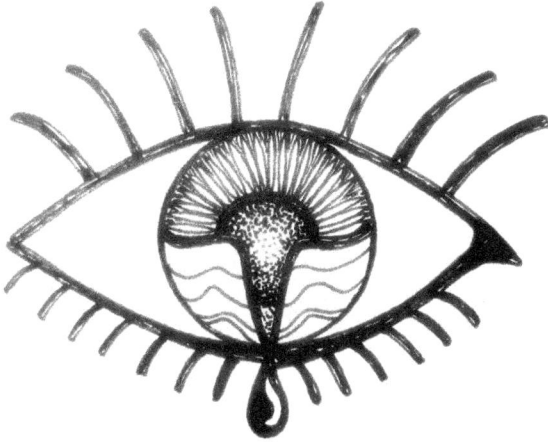

The EYE is my world. The ocean, a body of water flowing into a single tear from my soul. It's a physical emotional representation of my insight. It is the tear of knowledge and strength, and celebration of my journey that I'm about to share with you.

*Thank you Sonja from Soul Art
for this representation of hope, joy, courage, love and strength.*

From the Author

Insight shares my own first-hand experiences and a lifetime of observation, discussions, research study and education, coupled with the experiences of other victims. Names have been deliberately left out or changed for either legal or moral reasons. It is the right of every Victim to identify themselves when and if they choose to do so, and their courage should be respected.

TESTIMONIALS

Sexual assault is a serious and mostly unreported crime. Michelle Sleight's story is a most realistic account of what actually happens, types of assault, the impact of assault and the many likely outcomes. Child sexual assault is most pernicious and affects one in four girls and one in ten boys. The recent Royal Commission into Institutional Abuse tells only some of the story as most child sexual abuse occurs in the family.

In telling her story Michelle's bravery and honesty shines through. She describes how her life is affected by her childhood abuse, how offenders are protected by victim and community reactions of shame, blame and guilt making the risks of disclosing, or not disclosing, more acute. Her extraordinary story describing how she moves from victim to survivor will resonate with many and her strategies for survival are relevant and practical.

The biggest challenge is prevention and for that much work needs to be done to change community attitudes and the justice system. Michelle's story, and the information she provides, will add to the evidence to promote change.

Susan Kendall AM
Social Worker
Mentor PRADET East Timor

In this living memoir, Michelle brings the reader along on her own personal journey from Victim to Survivor. At times emotional, at times educational, this book conveys the experiences of one woman's road to recovery. Written in a friendly and generous style, Michelle has not only shown that recovery is possible, but that writing is one pathway through the healing process.

Professional therapist and clinician,
Brisbane Australia

DEDICATION

Insight celebrates the courage of all Victims who take the next breath, and then the next step, and the survivors who take back their lives. I dedicate this book to these brave people and the sexual assault specialists who recognise Victims and Survivors of sexual assault are important, and work to help transform Victims of sexual assault into Survivors.

CONTENTS

TIME FOR CHANGE

People may pick up my book and put it back. However, I believe the messages I share could set you or someone you care about free from living as a Victim, now or in the future. It may spare you, your children or someone you care about unnecessary misery. I spoke to a woman in her twenties who asked if you haven't been sexually assaulted, why read the book? She was shocked to learn the likelihood of the sexual assault epidemic reaching into her world and sucking her into a dark, despairing existence, at some point, is a statistical probability of approximately one in five women and one in twenty men over the age of 15 years based on reported assaults. Unfortunately, not everyone reports (Phillips & Park, 2006) (Victorian Centres Against Sexual Assault (CASA) Forum, 2019).

Ask yourself, do you really know about sexual assault? Is what you know accurate? Are you aware of sexual predator dialogue and the loopholes they create to slither through? Do you know it's never the Victim's fault? In my experience, most people aren't as educated as they need to be to help their loved ones, and themselves, should a sexual predator darken their lives.

I've written this book because of the current myths and misconceptions I've identified surrounding sexual assault culture. I categorise and discuss a variety of sexual predators, sharing how they get away with sexual assault. Most people can relate to the Classic Rapists while, in my experience, they're blind to what I consider the significantly more prevalent and dangerous Garden Variety. I discuss why predators sexually assault, who they hunt and why those Victims are chosen.

I watched a lovely young woman bravely share her sexual assault, via video clip. Being that exposed is extremely difficult; please appreciate how hard it is to publicly identify as a Victim. Sadly, this woman was perfect prey. From what she said it was clear to me her rapist had set a trap and laid out a defence she accepted. Having invited her over, she said he appeared drunk on her arrival. He showed her a cupboard full of alcohol, which doesn't suggest he was drunk but rather that he could use it as a show-and-tell excuse. His mood apparently became more aggressive during their conversation. This led her to think she had provoked the rape. Several days later when she confronted him about raping her, he feigned no knowledge. He told her he couldn't remember because he was so drunk. Her flatmate told her she hadn't been raped which she accepted. I see this situation differently. I suggest, like other sexual predators I know or have experienced, his drunk excuse was a familiar ploy he had possibly used before. His progressively aggressive behaviour led her to think she was responsible for the assault. Then he disarmed her with his lack of memory and shock. Due to her upbringing, leaving her vulnerable, she never challenged him. Instead she accepted his well-laid-out dialogue to get away with rape. One of my rapists used alcohol as an excuse. However, in a moment alone with me, after the rape, he revelled in what he'd done to me. He derived further pleasure from the memory, and my present discomfort. He described assaulting me before I woke up. He wasn't drunk. From rapists I've known or have information on, it appears they want to remember in detail; being drunk would inhibit this (Ladylike, 2019).

Are you aware of the Victim's automatic physical and emotional responses during and following an assault? Are you aware of the threat trauma poses to you or your loved ones? Do you know what to do if it happens to you? Do you have a plan? Have you thought about how to move forward when you can't think? In my experience people either don't think about it or think they know. Sadly, when a predator strikes, their world falls apart and they realise everything they thought they knew isn't right. In many cases this reality has worked against Victims.

Victims and their families struggle with the multitude of issues resulting from sexual assault trauma. Many don't constructively resolve the issues which is dangerous. These issues manifest in dysfunctional behaviour in their lives. This can lead to suicide, a broken existence or a miserable life.

An example of this is the death of a 17-year-old Victim of two separate paedophiles. She chose to end her life in a euthanasia clinic because she couldn't cope with the trauma. It broke my heart to hear about her decision ('Teenager who was sexually assaulted multiple times ends her own life after requesting legal euthanasia', 2019).

Another example is a middle-aged woman who verbally abused my friend for speaking openly about her sexual assault. The woman screamed, "Stop talking about it … it happened to me and I don't talk about it … why are you? You're making it worse." Clearly this woman, described to me as a controlling and officious divorced office manager, while successful in her career, hadn't found a comfortable, empowered way to live with her assault. If this is you, through this journey I'll show you there is a healthier way forward. Please never underestimate the severity of sexual assault trauma.

When I talk about being sexually assaulted, many people become uncomfortable, shocked or unsure how to respond. Others identify and share their story, sometimes for the first time. I look forward to a time when this topic can be discussed responsibly, when, as a society, we're more accepting, supportive and comfortable talking openly about sexual assault.

It is my experience many parents still have no idea how to cope when their child is sexually assaulted, being harassed or stalked. I advocate parents need two plans. One plan to responsibly educate their children about consensual sex and sexual predators. The other is a survival plan for themselves and their children.

I advocate having a survival plan is essential for everyone. When you're in shock, you don't think rationally. Having a plan gives you something concrete to follow if sexual assault enters your world, directly or indirectly. Otherwise, like me, you could be left dead but living. Check out some basic outlines to use on my website www.michelleinsight.com.au or other websites listed in my Resource Bibliography.

Another concern is society's response to Victims. This can be just as traumatic as the assault. Today's current thinking around sexual assault still tends to blame the Victim: "What did you do to provoke it?" or "She must have done something … it's her fault". Sadly, many Victims mirror this: "It was my fault, I did … I didn't do …" These typical responses undermine a fragile, traumatised Victim and send the wrong message.

Alternatively, and equally problematic, are the well-meant comments: "Try to think happy thoughts … think about what you have to be grateful for … don't dwell on it, it'll only make it worse." Victims I know shut up and suffered in silence. Personally, when these things were said to me, I felt angry. The advice is unrealistic and unhealthy. How you respond to an assault could be paramount in determining the fate of yourself and your loved ones. Are you equipped to respond constructively?

I believe through education sexual assault culture can be repositioned. Then we can collectively strike at the heart of the sexual assault epidemic. As a society we can begin to reduce the current epidemic, protect ourselves and our loved ones, if not from sexual assault, then from its traumatic aftermath.

Through *Insight*, I share a lifetime of knowledge spanning the various facets of sexual assault including my story. I discuss methods to empower you, the reader, and bring about change.

If you don't choose to share this journey with me, please, for your sake and those you love, find other avenues to educate yourself.

However, if you do choose to come on this journey with me, welcome. In turning the pages and reading the words we will share insight into this taboo world. My intention is to burst the bubble which is shrouding all the nasties making up the world of sexual assault and shine a spotlight on it. I'll share the tools needed to be aware, be prepared and be an empowered Survivor before or after an assault.

You may find your beliefs challenged, your perception altered, as together we open the can of worms that is the sexual assault epidemic. From my heart I celebrate your courage in coming on this journey with me.

WHO AM I?

I'm a Survivor. I didn't start out that way. I've spent many years as a Victim, living but dead. Sadly, I had NO idea. I didn't perceive myself as a Victim. My first reaction as a Victim, put up walls and never be a Victim again. This imprisoned me. I existed through the eyes and mind of a Victim.

My journey as a Victim began around five years of age. Having started life in Palmerston North, New Zealand, my father's hometown, we moved when I was around two years old to my mother's hometown, New Plymouth. I'm the eldest of three children.

I have fond childhood memories of living under my mountain, near the ocean, on five acres, with pets and my beloved books, like *Cinderella* and *Snow White*. Sadly, my most prominent childhood memory is of the senior relative sexually abusing me. He killed me. I was alive but dead inside. It didn't end there. Over my life multiple sexual predators have sexually assaulted me.

Following my two childhood assaults, my surroundings sustained me. My mountain, whether you call it Mt Taranaki or Mt Egmont towering above me, an ever-present fixture of strength and resilence against the forces of mother nature. The open ocean a constant source of calm.

The lights from the night fishing boats a warm, reassuring glow in a sea of darkness when I awoke from nightmares. Our animals, pets to share unconditional love.

Although I've felt dreadfully alone, I wasn't. I've had guardian angels. The first was my mum who is a terrific role model of feminine strength, resourcefulness and endurance. She painted our home, inside and out. She wallpapered, fixed things and was an amazing gardener. For years we were a single-income family and while Mum saved up to hire a digger, she started digging us a swimming pool. Mum could be ferocious. I remember when she caught the water inspector sneaking through the garden to see if we were filling the pool from the tap, she sent him running. Mum didn't react how I thought she should when I was sexually assaulted. This caused extreme problems. Although I didn't see it at the time, she tried in her own way to help me. Regardless, her influence on my identity personally and as a female was invaluably powerful. It enabled me to become a Survivor. Her resilience and strength continue to inspire me.

Sadly, I have one memory of my father prior to my assaults when he resecued Mum and I from my pet bull, who had trapped us in the whey tank. This lack of history and his response to my being assaulted meant he didn't start out as a role model, instead he evolved. He is an intelligent man whose struggle around a dominant mother led to a fixed mindset and an unhappy marriage, resulting in divorce. I watched him overcome his addiction to tobacco. He found it difficult; however, he persisted and succeeded. Now in his later years he is fit and healthy. This taught me if I wanted to do something, I just had to decide and stick to it. In my teenage years I remember him patiently teaching me how to drive. Watching him struggle within a fragile marriage taught me burying your issues leads to misery. The marriage broke up and through counselling my father found peace. He took responsibility for how he responded to me and apologised. This changed things for me and I made the decision to leave New Zealand.

It is thanks to another special person, our boarder, that I have healthy relationships with men and a loving marriage to my wonderfully awesome husband. In the few years our boarder worked for my father he was a positive male influence. He played Chinese Checkers and Monopoly with me for hours despite always winning. After the second paedophile assault, he was there for me. He never lied to me. He listened. He talked to me. He was kind, caring, fun and safe. I'm grateful every day for having had this man in my life.

Despite the trauma, life wasn't all doom and gloom. The good things sustained me. Mum was part of a large, close-knit family, my cousins more like siblings growing up. Although I lived more as an observer than in the moment, I have warm memories of piling into cars off for picnics at various swimming holes and visiting extended family farms. Annually for Guy Fawkes, all the family gathered in our top paddock, throwing their homemade Guy Fawkes on a huge bonfire. With smoke trailing towards the stars lighting the night, my great aunt pounded out the Hokey Pokey on the black-and-white keys of our old piano. We sang and danced around the fire, chased jumping jack firecrackers and painted the night with sparklers. Sunday tea was at Nan and Gramp's. It was a ritual feast of roast meat, home-grown vegies smothered in gravy and Yorkshire pudding followed by dessert.

Before tea, when the men came back from a boozy golf day, the aunts, uncles and cousins lined up to play 'Sheep Sheep Come Home' with Gramps in the middle. He'd cry, "Sheep sheep come home" and we'd respond, "We're afraid". Gramps would cry, "Who of?" and we'd yell, "The big bad wolf". He'd cry, "He's gone to Devonshire for seven years so sheep sheep come home" and we'd all run to the other end of the yard; those tapped would be wolves with Gramps. We had a 'Top Town' birthday for Gramps, based on a popular television show at the time. All the family and extended family made equipment for different challenges; we teamed up and competed throughout the day, finishing with two older cousins, lollies stitched to their clothes, running cross country and everyone in hot pursuit.

From the outside looking in we were a large, traditional family. However, there was a secret. Concealed on the periphery of my world was a paedophile. Over his lifetime, the senior relative assaulted several children including me. It's too often the case people compromise rather than deal with the problem and support the Victim.

For years I was the perfect Victim poster girl leaving me vulnerable to other predators. In my early twenties I realised I was living a reality I didn't want. This realisation gave birth to significant change in my life. I began a journey. Many years later, due to a different type of situation, I asked myself another question. From there I began a focused journey creating strategies to constructively rebuild myself, which supported me through another assault in 1996. Following the predator's guilty plea, I set a New South Wales legal precedent at sentencing in 1997. From there my strategies enabled me to transform and evolve stronger.

As a Survivor, I've achieved an Undergraduate Communications degree at University of Technology Sydney (UTS), using myself as my own psychology lab rat, and receiving a UTS Social Justice award for disability advocacy. My two gorgeous girls fall into the Gifted category of special needs which comes with challenges for them, and me, as a parent. I had to rapidly educate myself about giftedness, and how to navigate the minefield of difficulties I encountered within the national and international education systems. Another upright learning curve, in a totally different direction, has transformed my front room into the Cotonrun nursery, where I breed the rare, unique Coton de Tulear.

Within these pages I'll share my analysis about sexual assault and strategies to transform into a Survivor rather than survive as a Victim, from my perspective as a Victim and a Survivor.

Currently, sexual assault is identified as an epidemic. I believe we can change this through awareness, preparedness, taking care of ourselves and each other, and if necessary, transforming from a Victim into a Survivor.

STRUGGLE TO STRENGTH

As discussed, I use the terms Victim and Survivor to identify different ways of thinking and reacting to life.

Victims are obviously or silently living in trauma. They may or may not know they're a Victim. I think Victims are brave and it's important they value the strength they have shown to survive. When they're ready there is a way to use their strength and experience to transform.

Survivors are resilient, aware, prepared, caring and empowered. They're the architect of their mind, the author of their present, the producer of their future, with a purpose to live. There's always a constructive way forward for a Survivor.

Another term I use is the Living Dead. After each sexual assault, I died. My mirror image was a stranger, the face looking back at me didn't reflect my changed mental and emotional state.

In the Acceptance chapter, I discuss my methods for transforming from a Victim into a Survivor, based on my belief from birth our environment and experiences shape our thinking or mindset. Further, they create our subconscious default beliefs or automatic response and behaviour patterns. Changing my default patterns allowed me to transform.

Imagine you're born and as you grow your environment and experiences shape your thinking. One moment you're happily living life and BAM, a sexual predator attacks you. What happens next will determine your future. Shock is a typcial first response. Like other women you didn't consider yourself the type to get assaulted. Blame: "Why me ... what did I do to cause it ... how did I let that happen ... why didn't I realise ... why didn't I stop it?" Victims struggle to come to terms with themselves as Victims. Horror and self-judgement follow. Then the decision to tell or not to tell and getting help.

Victim A tells those they expect support from. That can either be helpful or harmful. Helpful is getting the Victim qualified and experienced help and telling them they're loved and supported. Everything else tends to be harmful. Support people, like parents, should also get help.

Victim B doesn't tell. Doesn't get help or gets the wrong help. Burying their pain, they plough on. Relying on dead soil to nurture and sustain them is dangerously ineffective. I know women who've attempted suicide, some have a trail of broken relationships. They're unhappy, lonely, continuous victims. When they look back, they often see a life wasted. They never realised their dysfunction was a direct result of unresolved sexual assault trauma. They're full of regret. If this is you, please focus on your whole life. When I removed the veil of dysfunction, I discovered there was a lot in my past, despite the dysfunction, to treasure.

Your subconscious default reacts without thinking, determining your reaction. It also forms new subconscious thinking based on the outcome of the default thinking and reinforces those beliefs manifesting them in your life.

Default thinking can work against you. One lovely lady I know from an all-male family couldn't tell her husband about being snatched and raped on her way to work. This lady's default was only a certain type of woman gets assaulted. She blamed herself because she couldn't reconcile why she had been chosen. Her blame and shame destroyed her, preventing her from getting help for many years.

Alternatively, it is just as damaging when the reaction is the opposite to the default expectation. For example, when the senior relative assaulted five-year-old me, I told Mum. My beliefs meant I had an expectation she would take action to punish him for being bad and take care of me because I was hurt. When Mum didn't react how I expected I formed new beliefs, such as I'm not safe and no-one cares about me. When I told my Nan and she told me not to talk about it, I formed beliefs like I'm not important and reinforced no-one cares about me. From that point subconsciously I behaved as though these beliefs were true and the outcome was, I wasn't safe, no-one cared and I wasn't important. This thinking trapped me. I continued to experience this in my life until I rewired myself and transformed into a Survivor.

Subconscious beliefs are repetitive patterns evident in our lives. In transforming, I worked from the understanding what others do to us, we do to others and to ourselves, in some way. For example, I felt others let me down, therefore, I let myself down and I let others down. One night I got a call for help from someone in a phone box who needed me to pick them up because some girls were bullying them. She was too scared to walk to the taxi rank. I told her to call the police. I couldn't come. Earlier I'd been let down, and in a dreadful emotional state, was letting myself down, contemplating suicide because I was useless, so worthless. No, there is no excuse for not helping. I could've called the police for her. I could've called someone else. I didn't. I felt like a failure because I let her down and the pattern was fulfilled. I felt so disgusted in myself about this I never directly let anyone down again; however, the pattern reshaped and continued until I transformed.

It's never too late to transform. Men/women tell me, "It's too hard … I've tried everything … I'm exhausted … I can't go on … I just want to die!" I used this Living Dead language until I transformed, creating a life where I see mistakes or unpleasantness as an opportunity, and live a life I choose. You can too.

COUNSELLING/COACHING:

I'm a strong advocate for specialised sexual assault counselling coupled with Group work and Survivor Coaching. In my experience, it's the most constructive way of transforming from a Victim into a Survivor.

Individual Counselling …
In my experience there are general counsellors and specialist sexual assault counsellors. Counsellors are trained to help people understand their trauma. I've experienced both. For effective results find a specialist as sexual assault trauma is extremely debilitating and difficult to resolve.

Group Counselling …
Loved Group work. My group held each other accountable, when necessary, and kept each other moving forward. We shared understanding, supportive friendships and inspired each other through our courage.

Rescue Counsellors …
Beware! An example, I was listening to a lady who runs a Victims support program. When I offered to come speak to the group as a Survivor she politely declined, saying her group wasn't ready for that sort of thing. When I asked what sort of program she was running, she explained she had no formalised program and was there for them if they needed her, they were very traumatised. There were no foundation skills to get her group transforming and flying her nest. Each of us knows what we need. Don't let others limit you.

Survivor Coaches ...

As a Survivor who's walked in the Victim's shoes I know ...

- The hurdles Victims face
- Where a Victim is stuck and why
- How a Victim feels, what they're confronted with and what can get a Victim focused on taking positive action
- What work to do to become a Survivor.

Because of our unique expertise, Survivors can ...

- Share their transformation
- Help Victims identify their achievements and strengths
- Help Victims plan
- Encourage and guide them through the grey areas
- Keep a Victim focused on their achievements and cheer them on into the light

The words of the Survivor who inspired me sustained me throughout court and my transformation.

For me the process equates to:

The past me ...
Sexual Assault = Victim (Living Dead) – healthy supports = Victim

The transformation ...
Sexual Assault = Victim (Living Dead) + healthy supports = Survivor

VICTIM:

I excelled at being a Victim. I didn't know I was a Victim existing entrenched in judgement, dreadful self-talk, self-blame, lack of self-respect, wallowing in self-pity and self-loathing. Some days I struggled to take the next breath; at other times I'd freeze for no reason. I was a functioning Victim; on the surface all smiles or depressed and hiding away. All the time drowning in a writhing pool of flashbacks, anxiety and self-destruction.

Immediately at Ground Zero, when the assault was happening, like me, other Victims describe losing their identity. We felt numb, lost, alone, terrified, barely existing. After the sexual assault, self-talk is a Victim's worst enemy. I punished myself with "I'm dirty, powerless and abandoned because no-one wants to deal with what happened to me, they don't love me, no-one cares". Victims describe feeling ashamed. Victims knowingly or unknowingly self-harm, indulge in reckless behaviour or try to bury it. I've seen Victims struggle as their knowledge and beliefs around sexual assault collide with reality. Nothing makes sense, breeding feelings of stupidity and judgement, leading to self-loathing, which was my best friend for a long time.

Left unchecked, like other Victims, I spiralled into self-criticism, self-hatred, fearful of rejection and being unloved. Disconnected, I became an observer of life, while operating from an emotionally defensive position. Subconsciously, my behaviour provoked outcomes reinforcing these beliefs. It fed acceptance that I'd always be hurt, never loved or safe; in essence, I was worthless.

Many Victims, lacking understanding of sexual assault, are sucked into believing sexual predators' carefully constructed lies. Lies predators use to blame their prey. They believe it was a mistake, a misunderstanding, they somehow caused it, or are convinced through their behaviour they gave consent, which is not true. Consent is freely given without duress, never implied or assumed. You don't have to say NO, you have to say YES.

Understand, like me, Victims don't always realise they're Victims. Fear prevents many Victims identifying themselves. Keeping their struggles from work colleagues, social environments or even friends and family. Many try to blank it out, experiencing flashbacks and awkward emotional experiences, making no sense to their community, creating misperception and walls. This was me. I'd turn up for a family event then drive off for no apparent reason. I left because I wanted to bawl my eyes out, tear the monsters out of me and scream. I was falling apart inside, and I couldn't breathe because of the intense flashbacks. This caused estrangement as no one understood.

Considering the number of Victims who don't identify being sexually assaulted, and the staggering number who do, Victims are all around us. They're in the workplace, on the end of the phone, in line for a coffee. Be aware, kind and patient with people who are struggling. It could be because they're sexual assault Victims, which isn't their fault. Please don't punish them through impatience or frustration.

Some aren't obvious Victims. Successful in business, not in their personal lives. Others committed to family, always self-sacrificing with no connection to their needs. Alternatively, happy, healthy homes and unhappy in their work or obviously dysfunctional, struggling with various forms of addiction. Please don't judge; remember, we all cope differently. To me, the saying 'Don't blame your childhood/ an event' is so ignorant.

Working hard to transform in 1998 I took the next step in my plan. Talk about jumping in at the deep end. I'd just got through setting a 1997 legal precedent at sentencing and I began my undergraduate degree at university. Often, I'd spend break time in a corner, crying to deal with a panic attack. If the attacks hit when out shopping, I'd be up against a set of traffic lights, or huddled in the corner of a building, crying as a panic attack swept over me. So many people looked at me with disdain, when a kind word would have made all the difference.

Over the years I've found myself talking to people I knew were silently struggling. When I asked a lady in the public bathroom of a shopping centre, "Are you all right?" she thanked me for noticing and caring. She said this made a difference to her. When a shaken teenage girl, months after being assaulted, shared with me her father's girlfriend had sexually assaulted her, I listened. I shared my experience with her. We planned how to help her move forward. This girl knew she was in trouble, being dysfunctionally propelled down a path she didn't want to go down. She was drowning in trauma she couldn't mentally and emotionally make sense of it. The nail in her coffin, her dad didn't believe her. It's extremely difficult for a Victim to speak out. If someone shares with you, they're not saying it for the fun of it, they're struggling and need help. Remember it can happen to anyone.

When I was working as a researcher at Channel Nine's *A Current Affair* (ACA) I had a list of support services next to my phone, to assist vulnerable people ACA couldn't help. My list included Lifeline, various government department direct numbers and specialised counsellors. I did this because I know how awful it is to be scared, to be overwhelmed and to feel helpless.

From early childhood, without knowing it, I rebuilt myself by default following each sexual assault. Life happened and I was swept along with it. Lacking the vital skill set, I rebuilt dysfunctionally, continuing the Victim cycle. I was a Victim for twenty years. Emotions governed my decisions and reactions, leaving me vulnerable. I felt alone, even in a roomful of people. I felt afraid and unsafe. At times I was hypervigilant and at other times threw caution to the wind getting drunk. I was repeatedly assaulted. My unhealthy subconscious need for approval and need to feel connected led to a work-related permanent disability in my mid-20s.

Arriving in Sydney in 1987, I worked as an office temp while looking for full-time employment. After being short-listed for a personal assistant's position I underwent a psychological evaluation as part of the employment process. I remember a shocked, unsure, elegant employment agent nervously explaining I didn't get the job. The results were non-uniform, suggesting multiple personality responses. I've always been aware, minute to minute, of my life without blackouts, so I didn't have multiple personality disorder. However, what the test identified was what I call the 'Chameleon Effect' resulting from sexual assault. I changed my behaviour to suit varying situations, to blend in and keep safe. I have subsequently been given a clean bill of mental health from Dr Darina Rich of A-Z counselling (I have permission to publish her name). There's only one author, so it's safe to read on.

Speaking as a self-proclaimed Victim expert, I don't recommend being a Victim. From the moment the sexual assault begins the prey is a Victim. I advocate, if possible, from the first moments of thought, Victims get on with transforming into a Survivor. Your plan should include messages to say to yourself like: "This isn't my fault … I love myself … I'm a Survivor."

As a child I didn't undergo counselling. Growing up I didn't know there were counsellors. When I discovered counsellors existed, I used them. If something upsetting happens in your life, regardless of what it is, please don't bury it. Please don't ignore it. See a specialist counsellor or speak to a coach. Don't leave yourself vulnerable. Don't be living but dead.

TRANSFORMATION:

In 1987, in my early 20s, I flew away from my home to find me. When I started to question, I began to awaken. I realised I was trapped in a dark tunnel looking up at a pinprick of light calling me. After an existence disconnected from meaning, unhealthy subconscious behavioural patterns repeatedly exposing me to misery and pain, I knew I belonged in the light. That light held the meaning I was searching for. I went in search of a different life. I knew if I didn't, I'd cease to exist. I remember sitting on the plane, for the first time, terror and hope my companions, as we climbed into the sky, bound for the unknown. On leaving New Zealand the self-abusive bulimia stopped. However, the flashbacks, sense of terror and fear were constant. Headed to England, I settled in Sydney. This is where I transformed.

From a shaky beginning came enlightenment. Terrified, I put myself on the line. Self-improvement and grooming classes with a former Miss Australia who helped me reconnect and feel comfortable with my physical and personality identities. It was drama classes which opened the lid on me, life and meaning. Desconstrucing character personalities from text and behaviour and teasing out the details to establish the truth was exciting.

I sank my teeth into drama class with a passion, and for years I focused on a career in acting. I'm happy that never eventuated.

Different types of jobs brought me into contact with a diverse range of people and I was so humbled from knowing the wonder of everyday people living their lives with love and consideration, caring and family.

The road to transformation was long, bumpy and often lonely. My desire to find a place to belong led to a permanent physical pain-related injury. Having worked with the company for some time I was temporarily transferred to an unsatisfactory workstation. Promises to rectify the situation were empty. The injury ended my ability to access traditional employment. The situation was terrifying. At times I couldn't put food on the table. In the early days I couldn't hold basic utensils. It rattled me to the core. I was so self-reliant and not being able to provide for myself tore my fragile identity to shreds. Despite being in dreadful pain, I refused heavy painkillers as I knew medication was a trap. I learnt to manage the disability and live in constant pain. I thought I'd been lonely before the injury; however, once I was injured, I was terribly alone and shunned yet again.

I asked another question: "Why do bad things keep happening to me?" I'd spoken up about having physical symptoms, I'd asked for another workstation and although I'd been promised a new desk no-one took immediate action. The answer to my question was, I shouldn't have believed my employer. However, my osteopath told me it would be all right if I kept seeing him. I believed him because he was qualified to know what he was talking about.

My question led me to me teaming up with a forward-thinking woman and working towards constructive change through years of hard work. I identified and diarised my Victim behaviour and belief patterns. Constructively, I replaced these patterns with more empowering beliefs and patterns. I grew stronger identifying with my values, what I considered acceptable from myself and others. Several years into this work, knowing I needed help, I worked with a wonderful psychologist to unearth deep-seated issues.

I journeyed into an intuitive world I'd kept to myself, exposing my inner diamond, an original part of me I was born with. During this time, I worked hard listening to my subconscious, what it was saying to me, what I was saying to the world.

I replaced negative behavioural patterns with positive ones. This journey of self-discovery was so powerfully rewarding. I prised out the true me to treasure, disposing of the dysfunction forced upon me. There were bits of a 'little me' afraid, screaming and bawling my eyes out. An 'abandoned me' who felt angry and worthless. The 'teenage me', thrown aside and blamed, who hated the world. And there was ME, who rationally understood why people behave the way they do. This ME marvelled at the beauty of life. I celebrated an insight into the special things in life. This propelled me forward with renewed energy. I believed there was something special waiting for me, and I cherished the special experiences happening to me in that moment.

Over the years I clawed my way into the 'light', only to be forced back into the dark hole in May 1996. Devastation struck when Mr Pleaded Guilty raped me. Because my years of hard work I had a Survivor mindset. I decided this time it would be different; I would handle things the way I wanted.

Mr Pleaded Guilty was my friend's husband. He raped me while his son slept in his bed, in the same room with me, and his wife, my friend, slept in the room next door. No compromise for friendship. I put myself first. I made a commitment to myself that the aftermath of this rape would be handled according to what was best for me.

I was a broken Survivor not a Victim. With help and determination this experience left me stronger, although the horror has never left me. Following the assault, with help from a dear friend, who I'm grateful to every day of my life, I ended up at Westmead Hospital. From there I found myself in the experienced, nurturing, safe hands of an amazing woman, Susan Kendall (I have permission to publish her name), and her team at the Royal North Shore Sexual Assault Unit. It was there I began constructively rebuilding myself again, with the help of a caring, experienced sexual assault team. This is when I sank my teeth into my formalised education about understanding sexual assault trauma and sexual predators from a research perspective.

Without Susan, and the team's expertise in this area, I wouldn't be who I am today. Sadly, vital services like this appear to be in short supply and significantly understaffed given Australia's current epidemic. This needs to change.

I reported the assault to police, and with the help of Susan Kendall and my counsellor, I set the legal precedent.

On returning to Australia in 2012, from living abroad due to my husband's work, I experienced heightened symptoms. In 2013, I reached out to Susan who was working part time with the Royal North Shore Hospital, and in East Timor with sexual assault victims. Susan is now a social worker and international mentor and has been an incredible source of encouragement and support to me. Susan explained that as my children reached the ages I'd been sexually abused, this would affect me, as would returning to Australia. Thanks to Susan I knew I needed further support. Apparently, re-attending sexual assault counselling isn't unusual over a Survivor's lifetime. If it keeps my monsters at bay and stops me from drowning in past trauma, I am happy to reach out for help. I started working with sexual assault specialist Dr Darina Rich of A-Z Counselling Services who I highly recommend. Together, we added to my bag of Survivor skills.

SURVIVOR:

After the 1996 assault I began the journey to Survivor again, with a knowledgeable, determined mindset and specialist help, on my terms. I made it into the light, with more survival tools at my disposal. I've been extremely blessed to work with extraordinarily gifted sexual assault counsellors, being part of a Group and spending time with a Survivor. This enabled me to become a 'Sexual Assault Survivor'. Long title, one important word: Survivor!

November 2010, my Survivor foundation was put to the test. I was trapped in a rectangular bathroom on the toilet. Having forced his way in, this experienced predator was blocking the exit. Although I wasn't happy about the situation, I felt internally strong and calm. I knew if raped, I'd survive. He was stronger than me and I knew what he was going to do, but I wasn't powerless. I was aware, prepared and had taken care of myself, therefore not the frightened, vulnerable prey he was used to. This stopped him. He turned tail and left.

Having risen from the ashes, when I look back at the desperately terrified, alone girl in the dark tunnel, trying to reach the ever-distant light, I'm proud of her. I'm proud of her refusal to give up, her refusal to accept other people's limitations, her refusal to accept blame. I celebrate her constant search for a way forward. There were days when I was desperately depressed; I remember angrily berating myself because I couldn't commit suicide and make it all stop. It wasn't fear of death that prevented me from killing myself, it was knowing what had happened wasn't my fault that kept me alive. I would say to myself, "They've taken everything else, why should they take my life, my future?"

I saw hope for my future in other people's happiness. I remember seeing something, or hearing something, I would store away as a special memory to inspire me, give me hope. I found 'special' in the simplest of things. Special was the smell of the roses in the garden not far from where I lived in Drummoyne. Special was in the shape of a cloud, the colour of the sky and the sounds of others' laughter, often bringing tears to my eyes. I continue to find special.

I experience being a Survivor as being whole, not controlled by emotion or consumed with fear. I stand up for what I believe in. You can judge me, laugh at me or criticise me; I don't care, I know the truth. I'm not afraid of what someone might do to me because of what I've lived through. I know I can live through it again if I must, because I already have, and I'm still here. The monsters have never left me; however, they don't consume me. I used the experiences to create a growth mindset and live enthusiastically. I focus on all the wonderful things I see and experience in life and look for life lessons in the difficult things.

Susan Kendall has a wonderful saying: "The community has the eyes and the ears that can keep women and children safe" (Remarkable, 2013). I believe this is true.

Through Awareness, Preparedness and Caring as individuals, communities and a society we can turn the tide on the sexual assaualt epidemic.

HUNTERS

Right now, as you read these words, sexual predators are hunting. Are they hunting you, your child or someone you care about? Unless you're a mind reader you'll never know, until it's too late. I taught my children sexual predators are clever because they don't want to get caught, and plan accordingly. The predators who assaulted me had dialogue, expectations of victim response or protection to ensure they could deflect or explain their actions away. Like me, you may not realise you're being lured into a trap, or you're vulnerable, until it's too late. Mr Pleaded Guilty set two traps for me. The first failed, the second didn't. In most cases, predators receive pity, shielded from blame, rather than receive appropriate consequences.

Understand, sexual predators don't wear signs. Predators mask their darker side from society. In their article, 'Understanding the Perpetrator', the University of Michigan cites Ted Bundy as a good example. An 'A' student, active in the church and volunteering, Ted hid in plain sight (Sexual Assault Prevention and Awareness Center (SAPAC), 2018). Like me, be mindful of this ploy remembering not all community-orientated people are predators.

I've experienced a variety of sexual predators with different requirements. Except one, they all appeared to have protection or an exit plan, a way of either controlling the situation, or setting the scene to explain their assault away without consequence. A sober Mr Pleaded Guilty tried to explain his behaviour away with alcohol problems. Sexual predators lie, and you need to understand how cunning they are to potentially identify them and understand 'it's never the Victim's fault'.

To make sense of what happened to me, I had questions. I found academic papers and research resources complicated, contradictory and difficult to read in the middle of a panic/anxiety attack. The research appeared to be limited to incarcerated men. Further, for years I searched for an academic predator profile reecently reading there is no typical profile making it difficult to classify predators (Sexual Assault Prevention and Awareness Center (SAPAC), 2018).

However, over the years, from the perspective of a Victim and Survivor I have developed my own predator outline based on …

- My first-hand experiences
- Talking with other victims
- Study and research
- Interviewing a few predators, I identified from listening to conversations and piecing together behaviours and responses to allegations like a jigsaw. Some threatened me, others were flattered I'd noticed how clever they were, or concerned I'd recognised their planning, entrapment and get-out-of-jail-free defence.

Below is my classification and outline of sexual hunters to date. Because my profile isn't fully developed I've placed it on my website and invite Victims and Survivors to email me at info@michelleinsight.com.au and help me fill in the gaps. If you do share, please include your permission for me to publish your information on www.michelleinsight.com.au.

If you disagree with my analysis, do your own research. There are lots of Victims sharing their experiences and resources available to sift through.

WHO ARE THEY?

I've experienced two types of predators: the Paedophile, and what I call the Abuser.

Paedophiles ...

Paedophiles are men and women born with an unnatural love of children. They have emotional and physical sexual needs of children around a certain age. Neuroscientist Dr James Cantor said: "All the evidence suggests that paedophilia begins in the womb (Kitching, 2019).

However, research also suggests some paedophiles are made. Apparently, as adults some males, sexually assaulted in childhood, will assault children around the age they were assaulted.

Paedophiles are hidden in plain sight and are commonly viewed as nice people. They are talented manipulators who groom or control the child, parents and other adults in their environment.

The Abuser (Male/Female) ...

I describe the Male Abuser as developing through life experience. It appears some predators claim their unhealthy view of women is apparently related to an inferiority complex and masculinity issues from childhood. Alternatively, others claim they're victims of childhood sexual assault. Further, there is a link between porn and sexual assault acceptance. Overall, researchers and counsellors seem to agree on one point, warning sexual predators lie.

In my experience, the above is credible. For example, I know someone whose teenage brother sexually assaulted him. He struggled with drugs and was emotionally and financially compromised. He went on to assault me.

I've met Female Abusers. Some claimed they'd been sexually assaulted. All denied they raped men, stating you can't rape the willing. Incorrectly, an erect penis was their permission, although some admitted their prey didn't want sex with them.

THE WHY:

Why do they do it? ...

Simply explained, Paedophiles appear to be driven from love and desire/lust. From a private interview I learnt some seek assistance through counselling to manage their needs. This is risky as their proclivity for children is illegal and psychologists are legally required to report them. As I know firsthand, others act on their needs.

Alternatively, Abusers are men and women who can't control their violence, many from violent backgrounds. They're usually men with anger issues, who tend to repress to the point where they must release it. They go out hunting to find someone to dominate or control asserting themselves sexually as a male in control. In my experience, predators show NO remorse.

On www.michelleinsight.com.au you'll find my witness's statement where she discusses 'Why' with Mr Pleaded Guilty.

Why Me? ...

Sexual predators hunt vulnerable prey. This vulnerability could be the emotional state of the prey or their prey's career, or location based. There are the premeditated offenders who have a plan and/ or a chosen prey or location preference, or both. For example, one of the premeditated sexual offenders who raped me liked his prey unconscious.

There are opportunistic sexual predators who take advantage of certain situations. For example, safely locked up in my friend's bedroom asleep at a party, my stalker was caught trying to break in through an external window. I know of women snatched off the street in broad daylight.

PREDATOR CATEGORIES:

Through experience and research, I have identified two categories for you to consider ...

Classic Predator ...

In my experience, its more likely a Victim's story is accepted where a stranger assaulted them, even more convinced if the predator used a weapon. Victims of this type of assault tend to report sexual assault because they often have evidence, and they can't be convinced it was their fault. Sadly, in my experience, this socially accepted 'true rape' identity is rare compared to the garden variety sexual assaults that society excuses. I'm a Survivor of a Classic paedophile predator.

Garden Variety Sexual Predator ...

In my experience, these are the most dangerous sexual predators. In my opinion they commit the greatest percentage of sexual assaults, and are the least reported, or found guilty at trial.

These cunning serial offenders utilise constructed sexual assault scenarios to muddy the waters, using false societal beliefs to protect them, leaving them free to continue assaulting without fear of consequence. Numerous times I've fallen prey to this predator.

Disarmingly, the garden variety sexual predator is usually directly or indirectly known to their prey. I've spoken with women who found themselves manoeuvred into a typical situation, alone with someone they knew well. Some had publicly socialised with each other, as friends, over a period. These women ended up 'Freezing' when they were pushed onto a bed and raped. Outraged the predator blamed them, convincing them they'd consented because they didn't say "STOP" or "NO", they didn't fight or sent the wrong message being flirty. This can be confusing to an uneducated victim. These victims believed their offenders. Knowing they hadn't wanted sex they blamed themselves for not stopping it. Spiralling into typical victim self-loathing and hatred they didn't understand 'Freeze' is a typical, natural response to violence, and being pushed, for example, onto the floor, bed, sofa or up against a wall is a violent act, which triggers Fight, Flight or Freeze and shock.

To me, the cunning and planning of this type of predator allows them deniability and is very difficult to publicly hold accountable, given current societal beliefs and ignorance. Therefore, these offenders get a free ride to assault again. I know three of the predators who assaulted me had assaulted before.

Drugs and alcohol are favoured excuses. In the two instances in my life where this defence was used, neither sexual predator appeared drunk at the time. In the 2010 Halloween incident, realising I wasn't vulnerable prey and walking away, the predator proceeded to get publicly drunk. I believe he did this to establish an alibi for himself.

HUNTER OUTLINE:

The following compilation, within the above categories, is limited to those predators I've learnt about, been exposed to or experienced.

Incest ...

The senior relative was the first paedophile to assault me. I remember the adults loved him! He was always outside looking after the children: "He loves the kids ... he's so good with them ... playing with them" (in more ways than he should). Everyone loved the senior relative, even some of his victims I've spoken to, because they were too young to understand. He addressed his sexual needs in front of what I consider blind mums, dads, grandparents, aunts, uncles and cousins, in plain sight. A cousin described a family gathering where her mother told her to go outside and play, the senior relative's out there. When she looked out the window, she could see him creepily touching the child bouncing on his knee. She hid inside.

I've spoken to many women whose fathers have abused them and mum didn't believe them. These women struggled with unhealthy sexual relationships in adult life. I met a brave woman in her 20s in a courthouse toilet. She had finally gone against her family and church, reporting her father to police for sexually assaulting her as a child. From there her father was charged and prosecuted. She was about to give evidence when we met. I told her how incredibly amazing she was saying: "Tell the truth," the rest was out of her hands.

In later years, many Victims of incest have recognised their dysfunctional lives are directly linked to their childhood sexual assault. For example, overeating, risky adolescent behaviour, promiscuity, multiple marriages, domestic violence relationships, drinking and adult bulimia are some of the responses they identified resulted from incest childhood sexual assault.

Within this category is sibling assault. Nasty thought, and parents tend to downplay it, shy away from it or turn a blind eye. Don't; it's serious and can ruin both children's lives. The abuser could continue the behaviour outside the home. Get the abuser counselling to help redirect their issues and find personal empowerment. Left without counselling the Victim could develop vulnerable behaviour patterns and misunderstand inappropriate behaviour as being acceptable. Take the Victim to a sexual assault counsellor and/or a coach. Don't leave the Victim trapped in the Victim cycle as potential vulnerable prey for another abuser. Step out of your comfort zone and listen and talk to your children.

I've met many men and women whose older brothers have sexually assaulted them. Others were sexually abused or traumatised by a friend's older brother.

Abduction, Imprisonment and Programming ...

Paedophile:

I have limited knowledge in this area; however, the methods to accomplish access can be found within the classic and garden variety categories.

In the page-turning words of *Scared Selfless* (Michelle Stevens, 2017), Michelle Stevens shares her story with this type of abuser. Michelle describes a cunning, cold, violent paedophile who held her for a weekend of controlled programming through fear conditioning, using physical violence. He formed a live-in relationship with her mother while assaulting and prostituting Michelle for years. I recommend you read this book.

I have experienced one attempted abduction. The police had visited my primary school, giving the students a dialogue of what to say in certain circumstances. I was confronted with the very scenario they had spoken about while walking home from school. A stranger pulled up on the side of the road and told me my mum had been hurt and taken to hospital. He told me I was to go with him. Like a parrot I repeated: "That's my mum there," pointing to an oncoming car. He drove off, gravel flying, and I was safe.

Male Abuser:

I met a lovely lady who almost fell into the trap of a master manipulator. She met him on holiday and he dutifully kept in touch, grooming her. For months he said everything she wanted to hear. He ticked all her boxes and then some. Inviting her to his hometown, his mum arranged a street party to celebrate their engagement. Coming home she started offering her special pieces of furniture up for sale because she was getting married and living in the USA. He sent her holiday shots of himself with other women, just friends. He created a need in her to please him, to keep him. He came for a visit. Later she told me he had demanded she set up a partner swap dinner, if she really loved him, his needs would be important. Fortunately, she had the strength to refuse. After his departure paid-in-full, pre-ordered flowers started arriving. He'd been so sure of himself, he'd excuted the next level of his perfected routine.

Another girl I met was mentally and emotionally trapped. A self-proclaimed Guru manipulated her into believing his programming. She was afraid to live without her Guru. Because she found him physically revolting, he had her taking herbs to enable her to have sex with him. As far as I'm aware she's still with him.

During a guided meditation, a universal Guru suggested I have sex with him to share his knowledge on the physical plane through his seed. His suggestive technique was almost hypnotic. I never worked with him again. I know one girl he totally controlled. In my opinion, through isolation he imprisoned her in their home. She was dependent on him for her existence. He used Guru nonsense to isolate her from friends and family.

Domestic violence also includes sexual assault.

Over the years I've spoken with a lot of women who were snatched off the street or abducted in various ways. Some were set free after the assault while others were left for dead or close to death when found. In these cases, adult women were the prey. One was an ex-boyfriend, the others were pack assaults.

Stranger Danger ...

A male stranger assaulted me at eight years old.

Most people I speak with associate this term with Paedophiles; however, stranger danger isn't restricted to paedophiles.

Another sort of stranger predator is the silent stalker. After attending an Icehouse concert in the university town of Palmerston North, New Zealand, three hours' drive from my hometown, I got a shock. At an after party I was confronted with a scary realisation. I'd been in danger without knowing it. A man from my hometown whom I'd never met or seen before struck up a conversation with me. He'd been stalking me. He told me his favourite outfits from my wardrobe and where I'd worn them. He knew so much about my everyday life and seemed to think we had a friendship. It was scary. For example, we'd eaten at the same cafes, at the same time, and he had ordered the same sandwiches. I hadn't noticed him. After this, I was extremely hyperalert to who might be watching me. An impossible task. It was a very real threat. I was lucky it didn't go further; however, I know of situations where it did. Never underestimate stalkers.

Acquaintances are also strangers. My eldest told me while sharing notes with a boy on the periphery of her group, he pressed his chest up against her, his body crushing her arm, and stroked her hand. She told him: "Stop touching my hand, get off." He kept doing it, saying,

"You're the first person to realise what I'm doing." She got up and walked away.

Pack Rape ...

I've never been pack raped; however, I've walked in on one about to start. The Victim had been drugged. The pack appeared reasonably sober. I stayed the afternoon, until the female occupants came home and the victim-to-be became coherent. I was shocked at who was present. Not men I would typically consider a threat. One had daughters of his own. When I spoke with them individually about it, each of them justified their involvement citing her promiscuous behaviour and past unsavoury associations.

On a 1987 Friday night train trip at about 8:30 p.m. into Sydney, slumped down in my seat, snoozing, a group of hyped-up young teenage boys came into my carriage. They were jumping over seats and high fiving each other. I overheard this like-minded group celebrating the execution of a carefully constructed pack rape. Their victim, "the stupid bitch", believed "she wanted it" and they "really liked her ... hahaha". On realising I was there they came over to me, surrounded me and talked to me. Terrified, I pretended to be deeply asleep. They moved on to another carriage. Asleep I was no threat and I wasn't their Victim type.

A very brave woman, Emilia di Girolamo, published her gang rape experience in the Guardian. I believe, based on years of research, education and an extension of my own experiences, this article shows a cunning, deliberate plan of grooming a 14-year-old girl with the purpose of pack raping her. Solely to help you, the reader, realise how cunning sexual predators are, I have briefly deconstructed the assault. It is not my intention to judge or degrade Emilia or her parents. She has generously shared her story and exposed her trauma to benefit others. I ask you think of her respectfully and appreciatively. I have not included all the text. Her words are in italics ...

When I was 14 I was gang raped. In October 1985, I attended a pop concert against my parents' wishes. By the end of the night I had been gang raped in circumstances similar to those alleged by the 17-year-old girl accusing several men, including Premiership footballers, of raping her at the Grosvenor House Hotel. The men who raped me weren't celebrities and they weren't even rich. In reality they were nobodies. But to me, a 14-year-old girl, only 4ft 11in tall, with very limited experience of the world, they were glamour personified.

The men, who were about six years older than me, were in a pop band, playing village halls and occasional support slots to bigger bands. They talked about a world I knew nothing of, a glamorous world of recording studios and record contracts. Their faces pouted out of photographs in the local paper. They were local celebrities. They were a gang with catchphrases I didn't understand, mostly referring to sex acts, and little hand signals that my best friend and I emulated and giggled over in the playground at lunchtime.

That night, I watched them on the stage ... they smiled at me, pointed me out and waved; I felt grown-up and glamorous, and important. I had been seeing one of them, Liam, for three weeks and had met Phil and Simon once or twice. Liam asked me to arrange to stay out the night of the concert. He suggested I lie to my parents and say I was at a girlfriend's house, so we could "spend the whole night together". I would have done anything he asked because I had fallen in love with this man who spoke of grown-up things, who said, "I can't believe you're only 14, you look so much older"—though the photos I gaze at now tell me that I didn't. He told me that he couldn't believe I was a virgin when I first met him. Couldn't believe his luck, more like (Girolamo, 2003, p.17).

In my opinion Liam groomed Emilia, befriending her, making her feel safe and special. I've heard of men making virginity something for girls that aren't special. Virgins were possibly their chosen prey, inexperienced and easily manipulated. Teenage girls want to be interesting to boys and this makes them vulnerable. Educate your children about how teenage self-identity can be used against them.

So I arranged my alibi and went to the concert. I wasn't plied with champagne but with cheap vodka. I didn't drink much of it and certainly wasn't drunk. I was never a teenage drinker. After the concert, the men were on a high, enjoying the attention of their groupies. I waited while they circulated for half an hour and then they came over to me. Liam asked if I would like to stay at Simon's house where we would "all be together" or go back to the fourth member of the band's bedsit. (He was also a model and actor and having a party.) I didn't understand the hidden meaning. (ibid)

I believe the discussion around where Emilia wanted to go next was their blame-the-victim dialogue. I've heard of similar dialogue used on other women.

I thought he wanted us to spend the night alone together at Simon's, so this was what I chose. This is what, he later told me, he took as my consent. Asking me where I wanted to stay was taken as consent to group sex(ibid).

These men probably preyed on innocent girls, too inexperienced to recognise the men were establishing their rape alibi through this deniability dialogue.

The year before, our county had been terrorized by a rapist known as the Fox. Malcom Fairley broke into houses during the night and raped women at gunpoint in front of their husbands. My father, desperate to protect his family, would stay up all night after barricading the windows. He was determined no rapist would get near us. I felt safe, with my father watching over me. That was what I thought rape was, a man climbing through your window in the night. I never thought it would happen at a local music festival, the first I had ever attended, after days of begging and pleading with my parents(ibid).

Parents, please, your sex education should include sexual predators, their tricks of the trade and dialogue. Lack of education leaves your children vulnerable.

I didn't think Liam would spend three weeks getting to know me, before passing me on to his friends. (ibid)

From my perspective, Liam spent three weeks grooming Emilia. Most monsters are right out in the open, we just don't see them, especially if we don't know what we're looking for.

I was taken to a small modern house. There was a black leather sofa, black ash veneer furniture and Athena pictures of semi-naked women. It was a 1980s bachelor pad, I suppose, though I had never been in one before. I still had a Pierrot duvet cover. The men said they were tired and that we should go to bed. I followed them up the stairs, led by Liam. When we reached the room I looked around, confused. I asked Liam where we would sleep. He said, "We'll all squeeze in together." As the other men got into bed, I asked Liam if we could sleep downstairs, but Phil was growing impatient and told us to hurry up because he wanted to sleep, and Liam jumped at his command, hurrying me along(ibid).

Firstly, during Liam and Emilia's discussion when reaching the room shock would probably have started to set in causing confusion and clear thought to shut down. Further, in my opinion, Liam didn't jump, and Phil deliberately grew impatient. This is probably a tactic they'd used many times before, because it's aggressive and disarming.

I left my shirt and underwear on and got into bed next to the man I had trusted, feeling embarrassed, knowing that I wouldn't sleep a wink.

The light went out and Liam started touching me. I whispered no, said it wasn't right with his friends there, and asked again to go downstairs. But he wasn't listening. He had sex with me. I won't say this was rape, though it was statutory rape because of my age, but I was uncomfortable and uncooperative, hating every second of it(ibid).

Emilia whispered NO; therefore, it was rape. I believe Liam never intended to stop; it was always going to be rape; these men didn't want consent; it wouldn't have met their needs. Please teach your children unless they say "Yes" it's sexual assault and "No" means "No". The men set and sprung the trap because they wanted to rape her; if she'd gone along, they would've been disappointed.

I thought that if I just let him do it, it would be over and I would be able to wait out the long hours until it was safe to go home without arousing my parents' suspicions(ibid).

She didn't let him. Confusion and anxiety, indicated in her dialogue, combined with shock disarmed her, as her idea of their imagined intimacy was crushed and shock had set in shutting down rational thought. I've experienced this numbness, it's horrible.

Then the light was on and Phil said, "Can we join in?" And Liam said, "Be my guest." None of them asked me(ibid).

In my opinion, very smooth, well-practised and well-executed pack assault. Brave Emilia probably wasn't their first or last Victim.

I won't torture the reader or myself with the details of what they did to me; suffice to say, I was the victim of a 'ramming'—one of their catch phrases. I was raped by Simon and Phil in turn, each with the 'assistance' of the other. To this day I can still feel the chill metal of Phil's nipple-rings pressing against my flesh as I was torn apart in every sense. I often wake from nightmares where I am having the breath squashed out of me, a huge weight pushing down on me and the smell of his aftershave in my nose(ibid).

Flashbacks are associated with trauma and don't come from consensual sex.

In Nicholas Meikle's words, like the 17-year-old girl, I "stayed for breakfast", though I didn't eat a thing. I watched them stuff their mouths with fried egg sandwiches and waited for them to drive me home(ibid).

A rapist drove me home and I was criticised for it. Never assume how a Victim should act before, during or after being assaulted, it's totally unreasonable.

I couldn't call my parents or go home early, or they would know I lied and, like many teenagers, I was scared. So, I waited and they drove me home. I ran a hot bath and began a ritual that would last for years, scrubbing my flesh in an attempt to get clean. Friends frequently joke about how obsessive-compulsive I am when it comes to cleaning but the truth is this obsession lies in that night(ibid).

In my experience, shock would have set in before the first rape and from there Emilia wouldn't have been able to think rationally. Until you've experienced shock first-hand, don't presume to know how a Victim should behave before, during or after rape. I know the many fears and self judgements probably colliding in her mind, with the pack on hand to give her their desired dialogue of what had happened, and their description of her role in it.

I was humbled to sit in an audience in the presence of a brave mother, who, in court, had to identify the high school boys from her childrens' school as being the boys who pack raped her, while she was blindfolded, in an attempt to remain anonymous. I've always wondered where they got the blindfold idea from.

The Ex ...

The ex-boyfriend/girlfriend rape. Based on my knowledge and experience, from a societal and legal perspective this category of sexual assault can be difficult to prove. In my experience according to public opinion prior sexual intimacy seems to incorrectly wipe out the word "NO" and need for consent. I've seen it used to avoid prosecution.

I was informally told because I'd had sex once with an ex-boyfriend right after I had ended the relationship, him raping me many months later was because he thought I wanted it. After months of stalking me and being ignored or told to "Leave me alone", I'm sure he knew I didn't want to have sex with him. Having visited my friend group, with his 'poor me' story of confusion, some considered it my fault. My friend group shrunk.

Ex-partners have held past girlfriends captive and assaulted them, or assaulted past girlfriends following social interaction. Their accepted dialogue, "I thought she wanted it" and "she likes it rough".

The Professional ...

This outline includes all professionals.

Paedophiles:
I've experienced a doctor wanting to give me an internal for a sore throat. Most people are aware of paedophile priests who have been exposed over the years.

Adult Professionals:
A medicolegal doctor, shielded because it was an insurance matter, assaulted me and attempted to force further sexual acts on me. I learnt this doctor was well known for committing acts of sexual abuse.

Black Widow ...

In my experience, there are three types of female predators.

Black Widow 1:
Paedophiles.

Black Widow 2:
Some have identified as having been sexually assaulted in childhood or teenage years. Others assault out of jealousy. One Widow I knew, very jealous of someone we both knew, manipulated situations to have sex with men showing interest in our friend. One man told me he had helped her home one night because she was drunk. He said she wanted him to take her to her bedroom. He refused. He helped her into the lounge, where she fell on him, pushing him on the sofa. She had her hand down his pants before he could blink. She then unzipped him

and raped him. He hadn't wanted to have sex with her and had told her to stop. Because of his erection he didn't realise it was rape. Susan Kendall says this is quite common for male victims. Being touched in a sexual way that results in an erection does NOT mean consent. He said the experience left him emotionally traumatised.

Black Widow 3:
These Widows are very dangerous as unsuspecting committed couples don't tend to know they exist. These predators befriend wives who are popular, beautiful and/or successful. They find vulnerability in the husbands and form nuturing compassionate friendships with the husbands who let their guard down. They rape the men. Then they manipulate the men suffering from trauma and guilt into unwanted affairs. Finally, they tell the wives.

A Shade of Grey ...

There are men I wouldn't classify as Hunters, although they have raped women.

I was chatting to a chap I hadn't seen for a while. He told me he had been in jail for rape. He told me he was so used to women throwing themselves at him he didn't confirm consent. They were being intimate in his bed, but he didn't ask if she wanted to have sex. He failed to check her age. She was underage. He said he'd accepted responsibility for his actions and went to jail.

Another example is when a drunk friend left a party to go for a swim in the ocean. My friends and I split up to look for him. Another chap I knew decided to tag along and help me search. I told him I didn't need him. This chap was also used to having women throwing themselves at him. He threw me on my back in the sand and pinned me with his body. I told him I didn't want to have sex with him. He asked me why not. I told him I didn't and that he didn't want to have sex with me. He said why don't I? I told him he didn't like me that way. He helped me up and we went in search of my friend, who was safely asleep in the car. The chap didn't ask for consent and if I'd gone into Freeze mode, he would have raped me. I saved the chap from raping me and from that time on he thanked me by hating me.

Never assume. Ignorance is no excuse. There is no grey, it is either consensual sex or it is sexual assault.

Sexual assault is being identified as an epidemic. I believe this is a direct result of a lack of education about sexual assault, what it is, and how sexual predators get away with it. Until we as a community choose to become educated, sexual offenders will continue to destroy lives, for the majority without fear of public or legal consequences.

As I've said above my outline isn't complete. Victims and Survivors please share and help me fill in the blanks. Together, let's use our invaluable knowledge to build a vital resource to help others and empower society.

KNOWLEDGE
IS POWER

Consent, Consent, Consent

It's all about Consent. With legal consent it's sex, without legal consent it's sexual assault.

Do you really know what Consent is? Do you teach Consent to your children? Do you teach your children about sexual predators? Do you teach your children what to do if they are taken?

In short, after discussion with law enforcement, and review of websites (Reachout Australia, 2019), it appears to me Consent is given when …

- all participants involved in a sexual act have said they want to be involved, and
- what they want to be involved in.

Consent can't be given if a person is …

- under the influence of drugs or alcohol
- passed out
- asleep
- unconscious
- not thinking clearly
- being directly or indirectly threatened, bullied or coerced
- under-age
- incapable of giving consent due to a disability

If society is to address the current epidemic, we need to begin through precise, consistent National/International definitions and education.

Parents' Role: What Are You Teaching? What Are They Learning? …

Parents are their children's most influential teachers; what you teach your children growing up will determine their belief structure around consensual sex, their right to choose and sexual assault. It will determine whether they have a voice and how they respond if sexually assaulted.

I believe parents need to teach their children sexual assault could happen to them, and if it does, it's not their fault. Children need to know how important it is, at any age, to tell you, their parents, if something does happen so you can help them survive. As teenagers, my girls know the statistics of becoming a Victim of sexual assault, the trauma surrounding sexual assault and the importance of getting proper help to become a Survivor. Anything short of this could be detrimental to them. I love them, so I educate them.

When my two beautiful baby girls were born, I knew keeping them safe from sexual predators was virtually impossible. From around one year old I began educating my children there were bad people who wanted to hurt their girls (private parts). I taught them to say NO. To know what was and wasn't all right, and if something bad happened to them, it wasn't their fault. I taught them why it was important to tell me. I gave them words to use to tell me. I knew these were the most important things I could teach them.

Growing up my children were taught health and safety rules, which were non-negotiable. One of these rules was to never question my decisions or ask for a sleepover in front of other people. I explained I might know a reason for saying "No" that I didn't want to say in front of other people. I told them about a teenage girl I knew who had stayed over with her friend. The friend's brother had come into their room and showed them his boy parts, and tried to touch her girl parts, which is very bad.

I personalised my sexual predator message, telling them how the 'bad' people had hurt me, inside and outside, when they held me tight, touched me on my girl parts and kissed me in a way I didn't feel right about. As they aged, every part of this journey I'm sharing with you, I shared with them.

When they were young, I closely controlled and monitored their world, letting the people around us know I was always watching. There was NO mistaking my children weren't vulnerable.

In 2002, we moved to Gladstone for my husband's work, when my eldest was one year old. I did a police check for sexual offenders in our area before moving in. About two months later the news reported a maternal grandmother in the neighbouring suburb had apparently kidnapped her grandchildren for her lover to abuse. Never think you or your family are safe. Be educated, plan for the worst, keep a close eye on your children and live your life.

My children were taught to always tell me everything because 'bad' people are clever. I told them I know about 'bad' people and I can tell if they're 'bad' or not. This was enough when my children were very young, with me expanding their knowledge as it became necessary or age appropriate. We've always celebrated the good things and talked about and hugged away the things they weren't happy about. I made talking to me a practised, safe experience.

I taught my children 'No' was a good word, and if someone did something they didn't like, they had to say "NO" or "Stop". We practised it. We talked about everything they didn't like, and I explained the reasons people do the things they do. This education has given them a voice, and they know certain behaviour isn't okay, to stop it if possible, and to always tell me.

I've raised my daughters to be aware sexual predators hunt everywhere. I explained on social media you never know who you're really communicating with and they could get tricked or manipulated into meeting up. Hence my number one health and safety rule: tell me everything.

As a kid I was nicknamed elephant ears because I overheard everything. Don't kid yourself, I wasn't the only child listening. Today, through technology, children are either exposed accidentally to inappropriate sexual information, or are accessing whatever they choose with no mature understanding of the harm it's doing to their thinking around sex.

Currently, there is concern about the effect pornography has on adolescent teens' understanding of sex and leading to developing pro-rape attitudes and a proclivity to rape. Further, younger siblings are being educated from their older siblings' discussions, following up with their own internet experience. In Grade Five, my youngest told me she knew what 'orgasm' meant. She'd heard the other children with older siblings talking about it and looked up the meaning. Remaining calm I dutifully started to discuss it. Horrified she told me: "I said I knew what it was, I didn't say I wanted to talk about it." I told her when she was ready to talk about it let me know. I've always been involved in my children's sex education and their sexual dialogue. Whenever they asked, I told them the truth. The amount and content depended on their age. Further, I've discussed how porn distorts reality, especially the need for consent.

I've spoken with so many people over the years who have no idea about sexual consent; therefore, they can't teach it to their children. Educating your children might mean educating yourself, to know what you need to teach them. Also, as a parent, how to hear what they're saying, or not saying, and know what action to take if any form of sexual inappropriateness touches their lives. For some parents this may mean confronting your own buried secrets. Effectively educating your child may mean challenging your own beliefs around sexual assault.

Over the years I've heard so many teenagers say, "Well, everyone else was doing it" or they got bullied for not having unwanted sex, until they do. Left uneducated, girls grow into women who've told me, "I had to have sex with him" because "he bought me dinner ... gave me a lift home ... we started dating." Childhood ignorance left them believing they were obligated. No, these women weren't sexually assaulted; however, they unwillingly engaged in sex because their parents hadn't taught them sex is a choice, not an expectation. Teenage girls and women engaging in unwanted sex can experience depression, and/or establishing other victim behaviours, potentially leaving them vulnerable to becoming prey to sexual predators.

It's clear to me, this lack of education around choice and consent provides sexual predators with a loophole, which they capitalise on. Many rape victims are told, "You led me on ... I bought you dinner ... You were flirting with me all night ... You invited me in" to justify sexual assault. The difference between consensual sex and unwanted sex compared to sexual assault is consent. The difference between a conscious choice to have sex or being forced into sex is consent. I've met women who don't know the difference, and view sexual assault as 'expected' sex, when really, they were assaulted. If you're a parent, are these experiences what you want for your child?

The following is an outline I've followed and continue to use to educate my children ...

- Sex talk—age-appropriate explanation of what it is.
- Bad people and what they do.
- Stranger danger including the difference between really knowing someone, and knowing who they are, only as an acquaintance.
- Teach children No is a good word.
- Knowledge. Why it's important to tell Mum, Dad or both parents if something does happen. Mum needs to say some dads do bad things and Dad needs to say the same about some mums.
- Body identification. Words like vagina and penis may be difficult for young children to pronounce. I taught my girls these words, simplifying them into girls and boys to describe the sexual areas of the body.
- Identifiable naming is important. A young girl kept telling people Daddy was in his shed last night. One day a teacher asked was Mummy in the shed too. The girl said "No, it's Daddy's shed." When the teacher asked where Daddy's shed was, the girl pointed to her vagina.
- My children were taught never to accept food or drink from anyone. I taught them to say I have to ask Mummy if I can have it and call me. We practised saying it.
- Teach them what to do if they're stolen. I told my girls about a girl who had been kidnapped and locked in the boot of a car. She tore off a piece of her fingernail and put it in the back-brake light for the police to find, so they would know who had taken her.
- Discuss strategies to survive if they're taken, like focusing on staying alive. Find ways to trick their captive and get away.
- Teach them if someone grabs them to make as much fuss and noise as possible, to draw attention, to stop the abduction. If that fails try and leave an article of clothing behind so police can identify Ground Zero, the place where they had been abducted.
- Teach children the difference between consent, their choice and coercion. Keep reminding them of this as they grow into teenagers.

- At an age-appropriate time explain all parties engaging in sexual experience/s should seek consent from each other. Beforehand discuss what consent covers. Men and women get assaulted so it's important not to assume, make sure whatever is happening is okay with the partner/s. Prior to intercourse ask for consent and ask again during intercourse.
- Make sure your child/ren know anyone can change their mind at anytime.
- Teach them how to responsibly navigate through the world of sex, without false communication. NO means NO, and YES means YES. Silence means NO.
- As teenagers, teach them to say what they want. Keep your judgement to yourself. If you make them feel bad for saying yes this can become problematic. They may start dutifully saying no and then initiate sex. This is a problem. It muddies the water, creating loopholes sexual predators love to exploit.
- Remind them despite the circumstances they have the right to say NO at any time.
- Teach and remind them consent isn't implied, it's given. When it's forced onto them or if they're bullied into it, it's not sex, its sexual assault.
- Teach them what consensual sex is and how to practise it.
- Teach them it's never the Victim's fault.
- Teach them their choices around media are their responsibility and what that means. For example, my girls know if they send images of themselves to anyone it's their responsibility how it's used, because they can't expect to control or trust others to be responsible in their handling of this type of media.
- Teach your children the rules around social media and be adult about understanding it's a difficult environment for teenagers to navigate. They don't have an adult perception. They don't see harm the way adults do.
- Now my girls are teenagers we discuss how someone interested in them should behave.
- We've discussed what should happen when they're ready to have consensual sex. Both their rights and responsibilities.

- Teach your children at all ages to talk to you about anything they're told, shown, see or hear, which makes them uncomfortable or confused.
- At all times listen to your children at all ages. If they don't like someone then don't let that person near them.

Parents, please take the time to educate your children—listen to them. Act and support them.

You might judge me negatively for educating my children to such depths; however, it's given them the skill set and voice to keep them safe from becoming victims.

Recently someone asked my daughters if what happened to me upsets them. They replied it doesn't because they've grown up factually learning about all facets of sexual assault constructively and this means they're more aware.

Ask yourself, do you want your child to be a victim? And, what are you prepared to teach them to protect them?

Parental Response ...

Always be aware of the messages you are sending your children.

For example, I was horrified to hear a teenage girl's mum sharing how all the girls in her daughter's high school year were having sex with the boys, except her daughter, who was being relentlessly bullied, pressured into having sex. Mum said the high school's headmaster agreed it was a problem, but nothing was done to stop it. Relaxed with a cuppa in front of her, Mum, totally oblivious to her daughter's stress, described the other girls in her daughter's classes as sluts, and was visibly proud of her terrified, lonely, desperate daughter for saying "NO", saying, "I told her you'll be graduating in a few years and you'll be all right". I wanted to get up and slap the woman senseless. This girl, clearly showing signs of depression, was living with the constant threat of rape. I've been that girl, in slightly different circumstances, and hearing this broke my heart, enraging me at the same time. Calmly, I suggested her daughter move to another high school, as she was showing signs of depression. I warned mum if she didn't act her daughter would be raped. Yes, raped, because there was no way out for this girl; the headmaster was failing her, her mother was ignoring her, and the other students enjoyed free rein to coerce her into accepting this was her fate. Given the circumstances, the girl wouldn't have been consenting. This mother's ignorance risked her daughter's safety while sending her daughter the message that she wasn't important enough for her mother to stop what was happening.

Another example is where a cunning male teenage stalker became more important than his victim. On breaking up after months of dating he started 'Poor Me' stalking. I know this one well; it led me to being found, torn clothes, bruised black and blue, hysterical in a ditch. The loving mum of the teenage girl being stalked called the police about her daughter being stalked. The police advised the mum that when they spoke to the boy about how his stalking was upsetting her daughter and her family, he smiled. The police recommended Mum take out a restraining order. Mum was reluctant to do this because the stalker's mum has a mental illness. This inexperienced mum, coming from a place of kindness, decided she would arrange a meeting, in a public place, for her daughter to tell the ex-boyfriend she wanted him to stop stalking her, and reiterate she wasn't interested anymore. I asked her, "Who's more important to you, your daughter or him?" This was misdirected charity. Her first responsibility is to her daughter. His mother's mental state cannot be helped by no-one addressing the boy's behaviour. Mum hadn't realised she was focusing on him, and about to sacrifice her daughter, who needed her protection. I explained failing to support me over my abusers had cost Mum and I our relationship for a long time. This mum got a restraining order.

If you're a parent, how aware are you about identifying when someone looks out of place? In 2012, my friends and I went on a picnic to

Formby Street Park, Calamvale, Queensland. A fabulous spread-out playgroup with lots of trees and garden, meandering paths and picnic areas scattered on the fringes. On school holidays and weekends, it's filled with birthday balloons and children. On a typical day, the chill had lifted, and the sunny spots gave warmth to a winter's day as relaxed parents sat chatting. Realising I hadn't seen my daughters for a few minutes, leaving them vulnerable, I went looking for them.

Walking towards the swing area, calling out to my girls and their friends, I spotted an unusual presence amongst the children. This presence was a slim, unassuming six-foot male predator with dark-brown, short, stylishly conservative hair, wearing a checked shirt, dark corduroy pants and brown lace-up shoes. My approach coincided with him striding away. Seeing him, my heart had stopped. I called out "Excuse me", and he looked back over his right shoulder, shocked. Acknowledgement hit him. He knew I knew he was a paedophile. As he made for the bridge to exit the park, I panicked, in case he was working with friends. I ran around the park yelling for my girls. Other parents frowned at me. I rounded up all the children in our group. The man was gone when I looked back. My yelling was the only thing surrounding parents noticed. They were totally oblivious to the danger he posed. I wondered which of those children he had singled out. Had he already started grooming this child? Worse still, had he already been close enough to brush up against his chosen one? Had he touched them? I imagine oblivious parents are a paedophile's 'wish come true'.

Although there was nothing they could do, I reported the incident to the police. Better to alert police than say nothing and live with the guilt of a child being taken as a result of my silence. If a child had been taken, who do you think would be to blame? The ignorant, unsuspecting parent? In my opinion, NO, the predator is to blame. Please be aware of who is around you, and your loved ones. Other children can't protect each other and wouldn't know what to do. Don't take your eyes off your children. We have sober drivers to get home safe; likewise, children need their parents' vigilant set of eyes on them to keep them safe.

One of the doctors at the medical centre we frequented when my children were young gave me cause for concern. His walls were plastered with photos of individual children sitting on his knee. He asked if he could have photos with my girls on his knee. I said No. He repeatedly asked. I told him I was sure he wasn't a paedophile; however, I was teaching my children not to sit on people's knees as the person could be a bad person. He didn't ask again. Although he hadn't done anything obvious I informally notified police in case another parent contacted them with similar concerns. Would you consider this situation a clue to be alert?

It has been my experience, over the years, parents don't always react how they think they will in certain situations. As a Survivor I perceive things differently to other people. Most people are good, kind, caring, responsible loving parents with the best of intentions. However, when people are confronted with any threat acting can be difficult, because of shock, confusion and being unsure of how to proceed. These thoughts can cause blocks.

One evening while my girls were at training and I was jogging around a sports facility, I spotted a man lurking around the area. Next lap he was standing in the soccer goal next to my path, shirt off, grinning at me as I passed him. He gradually moved closer and closer to where the girls were practising. Mums and dads were upset when he walked into the girls practice space with his shirt off. Although everyone was uncomfortable with his behaviour I was the only person to act. I called the police. My girls thanked me. There was no failure on the part of the other parents. Our natural reactions like discomfort, disbelief and confusion can shut down a call to action. Please think about ways to get yourself moving when confronted with a perceived threat. You could start with thinking about how uncertainty feels from past experiences, so you are more aware if you feel that way again. You can catch yourself and revert to the action you've written in your plan. In the above example, I called the police; they have the skill set and authority to deal with the situation correctly.

School: A Place Of Learning ...

School is an accepted place of learning. However, I believe the education system falls short in educating children about sexual consent and sexual assault. My children's formal education never discussed sexual assault or consent, until high school. They were shown a short 'Tea' video, replacing the word sex with Tea, discussing how someone must be able to ask for tea, and not be drunk, unconscious or forced to drink tea. It's a funny video clip.

When I raised the issue of not educating our children from prep in school, I heard, "They're too young." I was five or six years old when the first paedophile assaulted me, and not much older when the second paedophile had a field day with my body. This thinking places our children at risk. It keeps them ignorant, potentially supporting the Victim cycle. Children don't know to speak up and stay Victims, repeatedly becoming prey to all sorts of predators. I've spoken with many women who've experienced domestic violence, uncovering childhood sexual assault. They never received counselling, remaining vulnerable, exhibiting subconscious victim behavioural patterns, which attracted a domestic violence predator.

My girls have dressed in red and made a gold coin donation on 'Day for Daniel' (The Daniel Morcombe Foundation, 2019). This initiative was setup by 13-year-old Daniel Morcombe's parents after he was taken from a bus stop, sexually assaulted and later found deceased. I understand this day is designed as a child safety awareness day. I believe 'Day for Daniel' is a terrific initiative and love what these brave parents are trying to achieve. Sadly, my girls have told me year after year no-one really understands; they know a boy died. My girls told me there was no safety awareness or sexual assault education programs taught to them on this day at their school. I believe our schools need to be far more pro-active, and supportive of such initiatives, to keep our children safe.

Reporting ...

If you have a concern, or if you have heard or seen something you're uncomfortable with report it to police.

Whether in the past or present if you or someone you know has been assaulted report to police.

Susan Kendall explained its important to report to police as they may have recieved other reports about the same offender. Further, where the victim doesn't want to make a formal complaint, some sexual assault councellors, with the victim's consent, make 'blind reports' to police about alleged offenders, using their names. This means if police receive a further complaint about the same person, they're better informed and would be able to indirectly contact the victim to see if she/he wanted to make a formal complaint. In Susan's experience when victims realise they're not the only one they often change their minds. Susan said using this strategy police have identified serial offenders.

The Famous Three: Freeze, Fight or Flight ... (RAINN (Rape, Abuse & Incest National Network), 2019) (Harvard Health Publishing, n.d.)

There are inappropriate judgements associated with a victim's reaction during and following an assault. It important you know what these three words mean and understand how they work.

Until it happens to you, you won't know how your body will respond; remember these decisions are made in a split second, safety being the body's number one priority.

Freeze or Tonic Immobility is the body's response to a threat you perceive you can't defeat or outrun. This is the most common response to sexual assault (Atkinson, 2010). In group our counsellor explained in some circumstances, this response is possibly the safest option. It could protect you from being hurt further from an angry predator who must fight to overpower or chase you.

The **Flight** response kicks in when you perceive the threat too powerful to fight back, and your impulse is to run. To help, the body releases adrenaline to increase your ability to escape (Aphrodite Matsakis, 2003).

Fight is a response to your perceived potential ability to defeat the threat. The body releases adrenaline to help you fight (Aphrodite Matsakis, 2003).

Please, never second guess your response, or the response of someone else. These responses are made intuitively to protect you. Responses aren't indicators of consent, they're our instinctive survival mechanism.

PREVENTION: THINK AGAIN!

You can't prevent rape, it's a myth!

As discussed, sexual predators hunt and assault their prey. They don't want to get caught, so they plan. They construct socially accepted explanations. The more common excuses are: "She wanted it ... she was flirting all night ... she changed her mind after." They use excuses, like being drunk, and they rely on their Victim's silence. Victim silence, as I've discussed, is born from trauma, such as shock, shame, fear and self-blaming. Victims don't typically tell. Many tell months or years later. I believe we can address the current sexual epidemic if we constructively change current sexual assault culture.

In the meantime, what do we do to keep safe? The typical answer is taking self-defence classes. Many women think this will protect them from sexual predators. Although this may be possible in some circumstances, overall, it's difficult to implement learnt responses at times of unexpected attack. Realise self-defence classes focus on defensive moves, to help you overcome a predator when they attack you. Self-defence classes aim to make the defensive moves, they teach second nature; however, this takes considerable time and skill. Further, the Fight, Flight or Freeze responses could delay your responses, making your skills redundant. Regardless, please believe me, it's not the Victim's fault.

Over the years I've spoken to people who are self-defence experts, women employed in the military and police force, trained in defensive moves; these women were raped. Many couldn't understand how their training failed them, blaming themselves, because, like many people, they believed their skill set would save them. As I know well, and we've discussed, the sexual predator is a planner; he's planned to take you down before you can defend yourself, otherwise he fails, and that's not an option he will willingly tolerate.

After the 1996 rape I joined a martial arts school. Firstly, it was too soon, and I couldn't keep going. Secondly, I realised none of the moves we were learning would have stopped any of the sexual assaults I've experienced.

From 2010 to 2012 I lived in The Philippines city of Ayala Alabang with my family, joining a Ladies group. This was a terrific group, active in fundraising, celebrating Philippine culture and visiting lots of interesting landmarks. We had monthly meetings with vendors selling their wares and guest speakers.

At my first meeting, knowing no-one, our guest speaker was a skinny, muscled elderly man talking about how useless self-defence is when you're about to be attacked. He told us when you know, or fear you're going to be attacked, DON'T WAIT to be attacked, take pre-emptive measures to save yourself. He told us we need to distract the attacker, pretend there's someone behind them or wave to no-one; when they're distracted kick them as hard as you can in the groin or knee. They'll buckle over. He told us once you've got him buckled over grab his head and slam it down as hard as you can on your knee. Our speaker explained this would put the attacker down, warning don't leave the attacker conscious, because if you do, you risk them getting up and coming after you, catching you, and when they catch you they're going to be really "pissed off with you" and they're going to hurt you more to punish you. He instructed us when they're down, before you run, if you can, "kick him in the head until he's unconscious". There was a flurry of chatter in the room at this comment. Our instructor said he knew this group of nice decent ladies might find it hard to do such a thing. I sat there shaking my head; I had no problem doing that. I know he's right, it really is do or die!

Our instructor explained Attack is more effective than Defence, saying if you foresee an attack then attack before they attack you. One lady at the meeting had completed his course and successfully put his attack techniques into practice during an overseas Hong Kong holiday.

You may think his approach confronting. Understand that rapists have a need; they want to act on that need, they don't want to get caught, they plan their attack, they set their trap and wait until their prey walks unknowingly into their web and they attack their prey. As you will read all bar one of the predators who sexually assaulted me appeared practised, and I know most had got away with it many times before. None were stupid, they had constructed stories as their get-out-of-jail-free card.

I DON'T advocate any method or technique because there aren't any; take self-defence classes, they may save you. However, please don't get upset if your skill set fails you. No-one knows how they will react when confronted with a sexual predator or find themselves being overpowered in the blink of eye and attacked. No matter what your response is, remember, it's not the Victim's fault.

The threat might be right in front of you but there may be nothing concrete to raise the alarm. The only way to limit the damage is through planning, observation and awareness. True story, have you ever experienced those times in life when you're fortunate enough to meet someone you get on with, you click mentally, and a friendship is struck? On returning to Australia from living abroad, the removal company sent an intelligent, elderly, interesting and friendly builder to reassemble furniture. Over the following five years the builder did a lot of work at my home, from fixing leaky taps to building an outdoor pergola. We became friends, had a lot of laughs and over time shared life stories, meeting occasionally for coffee if we were in the same area.

Early on in our acquaintance, I drained my car battery listening to the radio while waiting for the girls to finish Kumon tutoring. The builder, doing some work at home, called to say he was finishing for the day. I asked him to leave the keys in the letterbox, as I was still waiting for Roadside Assistance. Fifteen minutes later, it had grown into a bitterly cold, dreary night, and he turned up at Kumon, offering to take the girls home and stay with them until I got there. This sounded like a great idea to two hungry, tired children. With my history I wasn't keen, but the girls insisted. I called Mum and my stepdad telling them what happened and asking them to go look after the girls saying, "You never know, the builder could be a paedophile." The girls were fine, no need to worry. Or was there?

A few years later the builder told me off. He warned that I kept too tight a rein on my girls. Criticising me, he said, "You stand over them too much." In my defence I recited their overseas trips with school, visits without adult supervision to shopping centres and movies with friends. His comments made me think. Although nothing I'd observed about his interactions with my girls had given me cause for concern, because of my history, I remained vigilant. During our coffees he told me of a past relationship he'd been in with a young mum suffering a mental health issue, and how he'd been a father to her young daughter. Again, an alarm went off in my head. A mentally ill mum means a vulnerable child. However, he spoke to them regularly, and shared the stories of their life with me.

While building our pergola, during a coffee break in the kitchen, he slapped the girls on the bottom as they ran past. I told him off. He apologised, saying it was harmless. I told him it absolutely wasn't, saying he had no right to touch them. Around this time, he'd bought my youngest daughter a bracelet for her fourteenth birthday. The following June he didn't buy my eldest daughter a gift. Although I hadn't seen him for months, and men are forgetful, this automatically caused me further concern. Christmas 2016 he didn't buy either girl a gift. The rare times he came in contact with them he'd behaved appropriately. Regardless, I was distant. In late January 2017 I was cleaning up my youngest daughter's bedroom, a necessary evil, and found the original bag and receipt for the birthday bracelet. Over $600.00. Not acceptable. I called the builder unsuccessfully to return his gift and end our association.

On return from my February trip to Hungary the builder had disappeared. His daughter and his friend called me looking for him. Eventually it was discovered that in my absence he had been found guilty of child pornography of a girl similar in age to my youngest, at Beenleigh Magistrates court, and in his 80s he was jailed for six months.

At his age, the builder would be a skilled paedophile. The awareness education I gave my girls and the health and safety strategies I had in place frustrated this paedophile and prevented him getting his hands on my daughters.

Although my children were raised with an awareness of predators, realising they knew a paedophile was a shock. I turned this into first-hand learning experience for them.

My doctor congratulated me on doing my job, preventing the builder from getting his hands on my daughters. Yes, I did prevent the builder from sexually assaulting my girls, additionally, I took equally important steps to prevent this experience turning them into emotionally vulnerable victims.

So, there are monsters in our midst, what DO I advocate? Firstly, learn from my mistakes. Secondly, accept we can't prevent sexual assault.

Educate yourself, like you are now in sharing my insight. Take self-defence classes if it makes you feel better, BUT if this doesn't save you, please don't blame yourself.

Have a sexual assault survival 'plan', just in case. Memorise the what-to-do-following-an-assault part of your plan. Make this second nature. Enjoy your life with awareness, knowing if you're sexually assaulted it's not your fault!

MYTH BUSTING

You CAN'T change your life to prevent sexual predators assaulting you if you're their chosen one, they plan.

You may be lucky and strike a developing predator, still learning his skill set. You can't know how you will react if someone snatches you or assaults you. Further, if you're like me and have experienced multiple sexual predators, you may not react each time in the same way.

To explain why I say: "You can't prevent sexual assault", I've listed typical 'Keep safe' strategies women practise, or think will protect them. Sadly, the list highlights to me how little people understand about sexual predators.

Lie still, let it happen ...
This could be a good defence, depending on the predator's needs. If the predator needs a fighter, it might stop them or keep you alive. If the predator wants a Freeze prey, then you will serve his purpose. However, you may be a Flight or Fight person. Remember, you won't be able to think straight, there's no logic, no clear rational thought, there's just shock and fear, hard to understand if you haven't experienced sexual assault.

Hold my keys as a potential weapon ...

What are you going to do with your keys? If the predator is a man and you're a woman, he's probably going to be stronger than you. YES, stab his eyes out if you can; however, better to use your keys to collect DNA evidence, to use in court. In my experience predators go into a zone, totally focused on their need, and don't feel pain. In fact, I think some like it, so you'd have to get them early to stop them, put them down and then run like the wind. Having said this, the last time someone threatened me I told him, "There's going to be a lot of blood ... they'll know I didn't want this ... now get out!" There was a bathroom mirror I'd planned to smash with the soap dispenser and a towel rail I could easily rip off the wall for starters. My reaction deterred him; however, it didn't stop him sexually assaulting other women.

Check the backseat before getting into my car ...

YES, I do this. Better safe than sorry. However, if the predator is waiting for you in the stairwell at work this won't help. You can never be totally protected, so if it happens to you, remember, it's not your fault.

Always carry a cell phone ...

Good idea, that way you can call an ambulance for help after you've been raped; however, it won't deter a sexual predator.

Don't go jogging at night ...

Predators hunt all hours. You could be snatched and raped walking to the bus or train station. Yes, be safe, but don't let it stop you from living your life.

Lock the windows when I sleep, even on hot nights ...

On hot nights I lock my windows as I use the aircon. I've been sexually assaulted twice in my bed whilst I slept, and the windows were locked on both occasions.

Be careful not to drink too much ...

This is a good idea, I fully support this practice, as it might deter a predator/s looking for an easy prize. If you're sober or reasonably sober, they might choose easier prey depending on their fantasy. Wrongly, in the court system or just sharing with others, you won't be blamed or dismissed as confused if you're sober. Either way, please know, it's not your fault.

Never put my drink down and come back to drink it later ...

YES, this is very good advice. I've practised it and drummed it into my children since they were little. I had a drink doped once. Luckily my friend caught the boy doing it. Being careful of my drink didn't stop a man barging into my bedroom after I'd had a bath, in my own bathroom, and sexually assaulting me. Remember, sexual predators plan; you can be so careful and still have your drink spiked or assaulted a different way. Remember, it's not your fault.

Make sure I see my drink being poured ...

YES, again, good advice, not always reliable as you could get distracted. However, I've drummed this into my children since they were little. Remember, this could help protect you from some predators, but not all. If you're sexually assaulted, remember, it's not your fault.

Own a big dog ...

YES, good idea. I have five small white fluffy dogs and have been rescued from a would-be thief. If you're sexually assaulted when you're out without your dog, remember it's not your fault because you left the dog at home.

Carry mace/pepper spray ...

Useful if you can mind read, know you're about to be snatched and raped, and have your mace or pepper spray at the ready. It's been my experience sexual predators attack super-fast: blink and they've got you. Again, it's never the Victim's fault; don't blame yourself!

Have an unlisted number ...

Not helpful. Hunters don't hunt their prey through phone books.

Have a male voice on my answering machine ...

Doesn't hurt. Sexual predators often stalk and plan accordingly. If there's a man in the house, the predator could have a plan to deal with him or wait until you're alone. However, to feel safe in my younger years I flatted with men.

Park in well-lit areas ...

YES! I do this. It can't hurt. One reason I do this is pre-emptive; if the light isn't working when I return to my car, I know not to go near the area, and call for help. However, this practice wouldn't have prevented the sexual assaults I've experienced.

Never use parking garages ...

Useless. People get snatched on busy streets and assaulted behind garden fences while pedestrians walk past.

Don't get on elevators with a man or group of men ...

Not all men are sexual predators, and not all sexual predators are men. I spoke with a teenage girl, a victim of her father's girlfriend who had sexually assaulted her. Also, the predator hunting you might be in the stairwell or waiting for you to be alone in front of the elevator bank. You can't predict the when.

Vary my route home from work ...

Taking various routes home could stop the monotony of routine; however, I'm not sure how this would prevent sexual assault. If you're the chosen prey, the hunter would know where you live and work, as part of the planning stage of sexually assaulting you. Live your life, use the most convenient route home for you, and remember, it's never the Victim's fault.

Watch what I wear ...

Wear a chastity belt for all the good it will do you. You're the prey, not your clothes. If you're the chosen one, nothing you wear will save you. Yes, sexual predators can be attracted to certain looks; however, you should dress in the way you feel good about yourself, as you can't predict who's out there and what they're looking for. Never forget, it's not the Victim's fault.

Don't use highway rest areas ...

Opportunity hunters aren't the only type of sexual predator. I was trapped in the guest toilet of a social group member's home with other guests moving around the house and grounds. If you need to use the toilet, use the toilet.

Have and use a home alarm system ...

This can't hurt, it may help, unless you're snatched and assaulted outside your home. Remember, regardless of what precautions you take, you could still end up being sexually assaulted.

Don't wear headphones when jogging ...

This won't make any difference if the predator is an immediate or extended family member or visitor to your home, or the home of your family or friends. Live your life and accept it could be the one thing you didn't think of that leaves you vulnerable. Never forget, it's not the Victim's fault.

Avoid wooded areas, even in the daytime ...

I've spoken with several women of various ages who were snatched off the street on their way to or from work, gagged and raped behind bushes or fences while unsuspecting people walked past.

Never rent a ground-floor apartment ...

Not a bad idea, unless the predator is invited in or can climb and pick locks. Even if they smash the window the fright of this will slow down your reflexes. Good advice that might help: if you get home and there's a broken window, don't go in; if you're in, get out fast, screaming fire! Call the police.

Only go out in groups ...

This is good, as if you go missing your friends will start looking for you sooner rather than later.

Own a firearm ...

How is this helpful? Do you think a rapist would give you time to get your gun out and use it? NO, they don't! I've woken twice from the pain of being raped. Owning a gun would have been totally useless.

Always meet men for the first dates in public areas ...

Doesn't hurt to do this. Will it stop you being sexually assaulted? NO. They can always find out where you live if they want to assault you.

Make sure to have cab fare ...

This is a good habit to get into for many reasons; however, I'm not sure how it will stop anyone from being assaulted. A taxi driver attacked me, nearly killing me, to rob me. Importantly, having cab fare could help get you to a hospital after being assaulted. This is a good practice to have on your 'What to do if I'm raped plan'.

Never make eye contact with men on the street ...

Be rude if you want to, it won't stop sexual predators. Bear in mind some predators like timid prey.

Make assertive eye contact with men on the street ...

Be aggressive, it won't stop a sexual predator. Some like aggressive prey who will put up a fight. I fought a rapist who seemed to need me to fight with him and then submit to him, which I didn't.

Make sure my family knows my itinerary ...

This is important as it gives your family and the police a place to start looking for you. This should be on your 'plan'.

Have extra locks on my doors and windows ...

It can't hurt and may slow down, or stop, the indoor predators, but what about the outdoor predators? Also, this is important for property insurance. When you're dealing with sexual assault you don't want the cost of damage to your home and contents knocked back. Take sensible security measures, I do. However, remember if you are sexually assaulted, it's never the Victim's fault.

Make sure my garage door is closed all the way before I drive away ...

I do this. It's the least I can do, and it might protect me from a certain sexual predator, but not all.

Make sure my garage door is closed before I get out of my car ...

I do this. It wouldn't have stopped any of my sexual assaults; however, it may stop my garage being used as an entry point, and it makes me feel better.

Lock my car door as soon as I get in it ...

I absolutely do this because I have experienced a failed carjacking.

Park as close to shops, lifts, elevators and light areas as possible ...

Yes, I do this. Also, I'm aware of who else is in the carpark with me, where they are and whether they look out of place.

It won't happen to me I'm not the type ...

Wrong. Predators hunt according to their own needs and they cover all types.

Depending on a sexual predator's modus operandi and their experience level there is not much you can do to stop being sexually assaulted if you're their chosen prey. They will take the necessary time to plan, prepare, wait and when you unsuspectingly walk into their trap, you're theirs for the duration. After listening to one of my rapists relive raping me, I can say the planning and waiting was exciting for him. Also, some predators hunt in pairs and packs, making it harder for a Victim to Flight or Fight.

Again, I say live your life and do the best you can to be aware of who's around you. Take the knowledge I'm sharing to assess situations. Importantly, practise the words you might need to use if you're threatened or sexually assaulted. Have them on your plan and practise saying them. It could determine whether you exist as a Victim or rebuild your life and thrive as a Survivor.

ACCEPTANCE

We've discussed sexual assault is the direct result of a predator/s need to sexually assert themselves over another person, without their consent, how sexual assault is traumatic, that it can't be prevented and it's not the Victim's fault.

Now I'll share with you there's NO cure. I've never met a Victim who remained the person they were before the assault. There's no special Band-Aid or drug to remove the event.

Why no cure? I've learnt and experienced every cell of our minds and bodies have memories we can't erase. If a Victim does manage to block memories of sexual assault, like many other people I've spoken to, please understand the block is a dysfunctional state of mind. The symptoms are still there. The memories aren't dormant, they sneak through, often from triggers like colours, smells, images or sounds, bringing devastating emotions, flashbacks and physical symptoms or thoughts (Saskatoon Sexual Assault and Information Centre (SSAIC), 2019). They'll be evident, lurking in various aspects of a Victim's life and a Victim's reaction to a circumstance due to these triggers can seem to others as unreasonable (Aphrodite Matsakis, 2003).

A lovely, well-meaning counsellor once said to me, "Being sexually assaulted doesn't define you." The truth for me is it absolutely did. How could it not? Nothing can ever undo what I've lived through, wipe from memory what Victims live through. Don't despair, there is a functional alternative to living as a Victim.

Victims don't get to choose not to be assaulted; however, they do choose what happens next in their lives. Our thoughts drive us forward. When I didn't know better, by default I was a Victim. Once I was aware, I chose to be prepared, take care of myself and be a Survivor. This mindset kept me safe from the last predator who confronted me.

This is empowering. Now I have an enriched life I once dreamed of living; I'm a mum, a wife, daughter, sister, friend and I run a business full of new life, loving cuddles and licks. Having worked with people, empowering them, helping them rethink and change their lives, I'm now an author sharing my insight into being aware, prepared, caring and being a Survivor. This strategy can work for anyone in any part of their life.

If you choose to rebuild as a Survivor, the assault will be a tool to empower you not hurt you. My self-love, self-respect, and the knowledge and experience of surviving empowered me. Sexual assault can't be erased, but with the right tools you can accept it and use the experience constructively (Atkinson, 2010).

Despite knowing it wasn't my fault, accepting it happened, and accepting I couldn't have stopped it, made me feel calmer. I could trust myself. This allowed room for a new life, full of new experiences of my choosing. The kindest, most helpful thing I can offer any Victim is this truth. Accept the assault happened and use it constructively. You can internally love and heal, accept it wasn't your fault and rebuild, focusing on you …

- What's important to you
- What you love and are passionate about
- What life you want to create

At first you might not know the answers to these questions. As I've explained, Victims die inside; the trauma is so intense it completely strips you to the core. Don't despair; regardless of your age there is a way forward and the answers will come.

Use the situation to discover self and grow YOU. With the support of a specialist sexual assault program, which could consist of counselling, group work and a Survivor coach, you can rebuild yourself. Rise from the ashes a stronger, more resourceful, empowered, resilient YOU.

Regardless how hard someone has tried to deal with the pain in the past, I believe there's always a way forward. If you're struggling with the flashbacks, the memories, the pain, understand this is your mind's way of trying to help you deal with your trauma (Atkinson, 2010). Find the right help for you, learn from it and rebuild.

The following is an outline of the work I used to create an alternative to the Living Dead or suicide. I'm no-one special and I transformed into a Survivor. You can too.

We all have the power to change our lives. However, first we need to be truly honest with ourselves. Some Victims need to realise and accept they're Victims. Victims must accept they can't outrun it, hide from it or bury it. Then Victims can use the experience constructively, transform into Survivors and choose their future.

As discussed earlier, my decision to transform into a Survivor took a change in my thinking, acceptance, commitment to me, honest self-awareness and analysis, self-love, patience and understanding.

In the early years self-help gurus didn't help. Words of wisdom and catchphrases of personal responsibility infuriated me: "I didn't ask to be repeatedly raped … abandoned … I didn't ask for this … it wasn't my fault … it wasn't my choice … I don't want to live like this." I had a Victim mindset and I didn't realise it.

I wasn't aware of the buzzword mindset when I awakened and began to transform. I transformed using a growth mindset changing my thinking, believing I control my own destiny through evolving, learning and developing my world. I analysed and educated myself and expanded my knowledge and skill set. My conscious mind sets goals and makes plans; my subconscious mind houses my passion, drive and beliefs. Getting these minds working constructively in conjuction with my intuition was my way forward. No, it's not airy-fairy.

Self-analysis made me aware of the dreadful self-talk and judgement I punished myself with. How it shaped my perception of the world and influenced outcomes in my life. I set about rewiring my subconscious, and reprogrammed my self-talk, self-judgement and self-image. Having a more realistic view of myself helped me overcome my fears and allowed me to accept myself as a whole person. This process also helped me to value my personality traits and utilise them to help transform into my vision of myself as a whole Survivor.

I actioned this through changing belief systems, inner child resolution and developing self-talk awareness supported with affirmations. I'd breathe in and say, "I accept what has happened to me, and I love myself regardless", breathe out and let it go. One of the most uplifting, freeing and difficult affirmations for me to accept was: "I love myself free from judgement and negative feelings." Another was: "It wasn't my fault, I'm free to love myself". I cried so much with this one the ink spread across the page, like a light lifting the darkness.

Through this work I teased out the pain, judgement and the Victim buried deep inside, fuelling the drama of my life. This personal exploration was free of judgement; there was no Victim, no right or wrong, there was just reality. Me and my ability to choose my path.

Living on pittance, due to my work-related injury, I purchased a piece of art I couldn't afford. Money well spent. It was a symbolic astrological representation of me. It represents how I should be, with my male and feminine energy balanced. This image remains empowering and inspiriational for me.

I experienced truly amazing results and inspired to capitalise on this, I worked with a wonderful counsellor. Using light tracking or pendulum imagery I released residual traumatic feelings. For years I've envisioned my pendulum, watched it swing, breathed in a warm light, wrapping the unwanted daily emotions in that light, and breathing them out, letting them go, saying, "I don't need these feelings, I freely release them."

This work enabled me to remove my landslides, roadblocks and emotional storms. Today my bag of skills helps me fill in the ruts along my pathway. Now I'm a solutions person. My children often find it annoying when they want to simply complain, and I offer unsolicited solutions.

To this day I automatically censor my self-talk and monitor my actions and reactions because these are my messages to me. Further, I responsibly filter my surroundings and the messages being sent my way. I protect myself and my children from accepting abusive or inexcusable, irresponsible behaviour from others balanced with finding the magic in life each day.

Some Victims I've spoken to found they initially bounced back, were able to get on with their lives and then hit a big full stop. Routine often enables us to feel empowered, that we have a direction and we're moving forward, away from the trauma, until we hit a blockage. I know this, and during group counselling after the 1996 sexual assault, I was committed to absolute honesty. If I didn't feel any better, I accepted that, and spoke it out loud. If I did have a positive shift, no matter how small, I acknowledged it, and celebrated it. I was totally inflexible on this point; I didn't want to stall my transformation or risk falling short of being a Survivor. I allowed no pressure on me to 'feel better … to improve'. I drew a line in the sand, it took as long as it took. For weeks I would tell the group I'm no better because I wasn't. I was okay with my lack of progress, because I saw my acceptance of the situation as growth. I knew being honest meant I could identify my internal issues and rebuild myself into a Survivor.

I've found the medical response to sexual assault trauma tends to be pharmaceutical. For me this didn't work. Twice I took antidepressants. The first time aged around twenty, I took one tablet, putting me into a dead sleep. This left me totally unconsciously vulnerable, and I overslept, making me late for work. I threw them away, deciding bulimia was a safer option. In 1997, I took a non-addictive form of antidepressant for a week and stopped. For me, a total waste of time. It didn't change how I felt. I knew, for me, medication was another trap. It wouldn't allow me to grow, to strengthen, to develop my tools to combat the monsters and memories. It couldn't help me transform into a Survivor.

I accepted the truth, what was forcibly done to me, mourned, started being kind to myself, loving myself, and focused on working to rebuild me, with experienced support. Not easy; however, empowering, rewarding me with a healthy mindset change. From a shrivelled plant given water, fertilised soil and love, I blossomed. Please remember to celebrate your courage, regardless of any back steps, because this road isn't all plain sailing.

Among many other things, myself and other victims of sexual assault have experienced:

- Depression
- Anxiety
- Attachment issues
- Personality disruption
- Addictions
- Post-traumatic stress disorder
- Fatigue
- Hypervigilance
- Poor concentration
- Self-injury behaviours

- Poor nutrition—weight gain or weight loss
- Suicidal thoughts and suicide
- Formation of unhealthy friendship/relationships

I lived with many of those scary words as part of my everyday existence. Currently I identify as having post-traumatic stress disorder, and that's okay. People are shocked when I tell them, saying I seem so strong. I'm strong because I'm a Survivor.

After the 1996 sexual assault I worked with the Royal North Shore Hospital (RNSH) Sexual Assault Unit. This consisted of individual and group therapy. This specialised, focused sexual assault counselling service was safe, empowering and successful. Here I again transformed. Not until my work in 2013 with sexual assault specialist Dr Darina Rich of A-Z Counselling have I experienced such dynamic and empowering counselling.

Dr Rich has a no-nonsense, focused, growth-mindset approach. This helped me ferret out issues and gave me skills to combat them. Other counselling, though well intentioned, lacked the results.

On reflection, I think Victims need the positive support of loved ones, guidance of specialised professional counselling and the support of a Survivor. Together at the RNSH my group supported each other. However, our Survivor guest speaker was reassuring and inspirational. Her words, her journey, her courage gifted me a real knowing of what life can be, of where I wanted to be, what a Survivor is.

Write in your plan a note to future Victim self about what skills you have now to draw on to get started transforming into a Survivor should you be assaulted. If you're a Victim write down the skills and strengths which have enabled you to survive and celebrate them. Alternatively, change your beliefs around sexual assault before you're assaulted.

ADDICTION

Sexual assault and addiction historically go hand in hand. When I hear people say things like you can't blame the past for bad behaviour, I think how ignorant.

Not everyone who is sexually assaulted will end up with an addiction; however, many do. Victims I've spoken to have identified suffering the following addictions:

- Legal and illegal drug dependence and abuse
- Alcohol abuse
- Prostitution
- Smoking
- Self-harming
- Eating disorders
- Abusive sexual relations
- Promiscuity
- Depression/anxiety

You may think I'm crazy including depression as an addiction. However, in my experience, from years of talking to people, some Victims are addicted to their pain and suffering. They always need negative drama in their lives. They're never happy or comfortable unless they can find negative undertones. Others are addicted to negative thoughts.

My addiction came right out of the blue, no warning.

I clearly remember the first day it happened. I was at a wedding, and during dinner, sitting next to my mother, the flashbacks became extremely severe, the voices so loud, the darkness relentless, the smells overwhelming, the memories of being touched sickening, and I threw up in the toilet. Wow, instant relief. The explosive pressure in my head went away, there was silence, no flashbacks and no disgusting smells, no-one touching me, hurting me. I felt calm, peaceful, even happy. Yes, my addiction was bulimia. Looking back, I'm sad for that poor, tragic me. Since my awakening I have reached back in time and given her hugs, love and assurance she's a special part of me, because I knew all that scared, terrified, betrayed me wanted was someone to care about her and love her.

Like all addictions my bulimia got out of control; however, for a long time no-one noticed. It was terrific to be free from the ghosts, from their smell, from their touch, from the terror, and the emptiness and loneliness that consumed my life.

My addiction went on for many years; I was a functioning addict and never realised it. I had no idea what I was doing had a name or was classified as an addiction. Yes, it's true, I had no real realisation about what I was doing. It was my secret weapon against my enemies. Purging myself purged them.

In 1986, I spoke to my doctor about my bulimia. He referred me to a psychiatrist, who prescribed me antidepressants. As I've discussed this was not the right choice for me.

On a later visit to my doctor, he told me my mother had been to see him about her concerns for me. I remember when we talked about it, she was angry. Although as a parent I now know it was distress, not anger. At the time I considered her response another rejection. In 1987 when I left New Zealand the bulimia stopped.

It is my belief the only way to ensure a victim avoids addiction is to have a plan. This plan should include a list of sexual assault specialists and Survivor coaches you can work with. After an assault get to hospital. Don't leave hospital without having spoken to someone and make sure you have an appointment to see a specialist sexual assault counsellor within 24 hours. Find a coach you can work with and call when you need to.

You might think you'd never have an addiction. You don't know how you will react following sexual assault until it happens to you. Have a plan to get you moving in the right direction, rather than risk going down the road of victim addiction.

IT'S JUST SEX, WHAT'S THE BIG FUSS?

It's true, a lot of people think this!

The big fuss is No Consent, it's not sex.

I know, firsthand, sexual assault is nothing like sex. If you're not a sexual perpetrator, have no firsthand experience or background in sexual assault, how do you understand the difference? I've asked many people, men and women, this question. The answer, they mistakenly associated sexual assault with what they knew, consensual sexual activities. Mistakenly, they believe sexual assault is just sex. I overheard the police officer assigned to me during my 1996 sexual assault case say: "What does she want? ... Does she want him to go to jail or something? ... It was just sex?"

This thinking relocates sexual assault from a criminal act to a form of sex, rather than being seen for what it is. Sexual assault is a criminal, traumatising, sexual act, decimating one person/s for the sole purpose of empowering the other/s.

In my mid to late teens I knew what sexual assault was, but I had no idea what sex was. As an observer I'd listened to lots of girls talk about consensual sex and decided from a scientific perspective I needed to experience it to better understand sexual predators.

With my girlfriend's help, I interviewed lots of girls in the women's toilets at pubs and discos to find a safe, decent partner. We went back to his place and he proved to be a good choice.

From arriving at his home to the completion of the encounter he continually checked I was happy and wanted to continue. This was a great experience for me because it was textbook exactly what consensual sex should be. Leading up to sex he asked if I wanted to have sex, and during sex we talked about it being what I wanted, with him asking if I was okay.

I found sex different from sexual assault. The experience was safe, enjoyable, fun and I didn't feel dead inside. The only disaster was when he stopped, and I didn't know why. This poor embarrassed man had to explain it to me. Although I didn't have sex again for a while, this experience left me with a safe, enjoyable alternative to sexual assault.

It also began my informal research into men and women's thinking around consensual sex and sexual assault. I developed an understanding of the significance of sexual predators' manufactured stories. How they positioned themselves within socially accepted beliefs and covered up sexual assault.

My early consensual sexual experiences were scientific in execution, lacking emotional connection, which worked for me. Adding an emotional connection into sexual intimacy was problematic. In the early days I was extremely dysfunctional, unable to combine a sexual relationship within a traditional relationship. Issues like trust were overwhelming and so were the flashbacks. I've fought hard to have enjoyable intimate sex within a loving relationship. I'm happily married to a special man; however, the monsters are still there.

Sadly, many Victims never get this far. A lot of men married to Victims have poured out their hearts to me about this struggle within their marriage. Their wives struggled to have sex and were emotionally removed. This results from an unrealistic expectation that Victims can put it behind them and get on with life. After the 1996 assault my father told me: "Don't think about it and you'll get over it." He'll never make that mistake again. I know other loving parents have said similar things to comfort their child. Big mistake. They didn't have sex, they were assaulted. Because of the trauma life will never be the same again.

The big fuss about sexual assault is Victims are dreadfully traumatised. They don't forget about it. Being assaulted destroys them. In my experience, we might regret a sexual choice; however, it doesn't traumatise or destroy us.

Following a sexual assault, clear thinking is gone. The ability to compose ordered thoughts is gone. You can't make decisions. Therefore, I advocate being Aware through education, prepared with a plan to get you moving, taking care of yourself so your mindset and beliefs will support a constructive response to assault for you or someone you care about, resulting in being a Survivor not a Victim.

NOT SEX? THEN WHAT?

As discussed, sexual predators sexually assault to feel empowered. Without consent their violent need to dominate is momentarily fulfilled. Consent would prevent the predators fulfilling their need. Further, in my experience, being able to get away with sexual assault, leaving their Victim broken, is also part of their enjoyment. Alternatively, in my experience, men engaging in consensual sex want their partner/s to enjoy the experience.

I've found generally there is a mixture of understandings about what constitutes sexual assault, predominately focusing on women's attitudes toward sex and men's approach to instigating it. Many find it hard to see the predator rather than the person they know, not realising he's both, a monster and regular guy. For example, if he tried it on and she's crying and saying he tried to rape me, or he raped me, the response tends to be, "Are you sure?" They are implying this is attention she chose to misunderstand because she was confused. Society considers real rape the Classic category discussed earlier. The more prevalent garden variety assaults aren't recognised. Instead they're excused, covered up or ignored.

Current language around sexual assault doesn't help because it measures what is considered the 'seriousness' of the assault. Yes, I've heard that terminology: Was it a serious rape?

Over the years I've heard many people comment about sexual assault, describing different assaults as being violent or non-violent. During my university days I heard a tutor suggest when speaking with 'street kids' for an assignment, we should try and find some violent sexual assault stories. I was shocked at this tutor's lack of understanding and knowledge that any sexual abuse is a violent act.

Within the legal framework there are also measures and language to determine charge/s. The law is cold-hearted, and the charge might not sound right to a Victim.

As a community, if we're to end the sexual assault epidemic we need to be better informed about sexual assault. Our language needs to clearly identify sexual abuse and the resulting trauma. It needs to incorporate the fact that everyone is different and experiences trauma in their own way. Sexual assault shouldn't be diluted through evaluation. All sexual assault is devastating.

I've followed discussions around renaming sexual assault language. It's argued this will reclaim power away from sexual predators or make it less confronting for Victims. It is hoped new names will encourage Victims to come forward. Call sexual assault jellybeans, it won't change the connotation behind the name. It doesn't matter what you name sexual assault, unless society empowers itself through education, regardless of the name, the stigma will remain the same. I think it would be better to spend the time, money and effort on education and support, working hand in hand with Survivors and specialist counsellors who understand sexual assault at a grass roots level.

At this point I've explained the difference between consensual sex, remembered with comfortable feelings, and sexual assault, relived through trauma with haunting flashbacks of horrific memories, often shrouded in confusion, self-blame and guilt.

If you haven't already, are you starting to identify what sexual abuse is? Who the real Victim is? Do you accept it's never the Victim's fault? If you're a Victim, can you see it wasn't your fault?

Part of your plan could include a message to self if you're assaulted it's not your fault. Alternatively, if you are a Victim a message could be it has happened and it's not my fault. No consent means NO. Silence means NO.

MY STORY

This is my story, told according to my memories, my perception and my experiences. In sharing, I aim to help you understand sexual predators and the trauma predators leave in their wake. On my website www.michelleinsight.com.au you can view my 1996 police statements, witness statement and Victim Impact Statement. These documents are what Mr Pleaded Guilty pleaded guilty to and outlines my trauma.

I share my story to give you awareness through education. To help you identify if you're a Victim. To reinforce you can't prevent being raped, and why being prepared and having a sexual assault plan is so important to your survival, or the survival of someone you know.

My story discusses what happens after the sexual assault can be as destructive as the assault itself. As a society, we need to better understand what sexual assault is, and how totally devastating it is for the Victims, and for those who care for the Victims as well as knowing how to respond to a Victim and supporting them to transform into a Survivor.

Please be aware I've been as honestly transparent as I can, and you could become upset. Please, no pity, I don't need it, I'm a Survivor!

In a Child's Voice ...

My story begins with the senior relative, found guilty in 1987, the year I left New Zealand, of sexually interfering with several minors under 12 years old. The records are appropriately sealed.

To me he was a glass-eyed monster with a metal foot. To others, he was a brother, husband, father and relative. I've spoken with extended family who remember him fondly, while others remember him as creepy. I've discussed how a cousin remembers watching the senior relative assaulting a child on his knee. I remember being trapped on that knee.

I was young, around five or six years old; he was sitting on a swing set with me sitting on his knee. It was a sunny Inglewood day with Mt Egmont/Mt Taranaki standing proud and strong above me, free from the clouds. However, I wasn't free. I was trapped in his arms, like a rabbit in the jaws of a metal snare. His fingers touching me, there was a rubbing movement with something hard. I remember his stink and hearing his jagged breathing as it heavily hit the back of my neck. These ever-present memories have haunted me, lurking in the shadows, flashing back unpredictably, always terrifying.

When I think back to this memory, I'm very sad for the little girl that was me. All the potential I had, all the possibilities of who I might have been, what I might have achieved died that day. I wanted to scream but the words got stuck in my throat. I wanted to run away but I couldn't move. I froze, which is a common response to sexual assault. I knew what he was doing to me was wrong.

Over the years I've searched my memories as there are many blanks. I can remember what he did. I can't remember who else was there, why I was there or where I was, other than the sense of a garden and the swing set.

I've learnt, like other paedophiles, the senior relative chose victims from families that were distracted, and my parents didn't have the best marriage. For me, it could have been during the birth of my sister while staying with family, or at an extended family gathering, because good old senior relative was always there, ready to watch the kids, bouncing one of them on his knee. It sickened me to watch him doing to others what he did to me. I always kept my distance.

Because of my early experience, I became what has been described to me as an overly sexualised child. It was a traumatic, profound experience burnt into my memory with lots of questions I've unsuccessfully searched my memories to answer.

During Sunday night's family tea while the adults were playing canasta, after Doctor Who had narrowly defeated the Daleks, I'd sneak down to the bottom yard and crawl through a small window into Gramp's garage. I'd stand alone in the dark dankness of it. A green-eyed, fair-skinned, short, skinny blonde child no-one missed, no longer innocent, shrouded in fear, battling the memories swamping me, trying desperately to remember the day the senior relative destroyed me. "Why was I there? ... Who else was there? ... How had he managed to trap me on his knee and why hadn't someone noticed?"

I'd also searched for who I'd been before he killed me; I had no recollection of me before his assault. He filled his unquenchable thirst and left me a barren vessel, a member of the Living Dead. I was a broken, lonely shell who understood he'd done a bad thing to me, changing me, and that realisation was terrifying. I remember H.R. Puff 'n Stuff and his friends outwitting Witchie Poo, who left our television screen entering my nightmares. Nightmares I was ill-equipped to cope with. Sometimes Witchiepoo was chasing me, but it was something more terrifying that caught me, and I'd wake with a start, petrified. Sally Field was a flying nun who taught me in my nightmares to fly, to escape. This manifested in my reality and I would often stand on the roof of our farm shed and when the wind blew stronger with my arms spread wide, I'd think about stepping off the roof, unsure if the wind would lift me. I never stepped off. The memories haunted me. Over the years, in my Gramp's garage, I mourned the potential that existed for me at my birth, gone, wiped out in one foul act, lost forever, leaving behind a Victim that no-one rescued.

Unlike most young sexual assault Victims, I told. I told my mum what had happened to me, and her response was to tell me not to be silly. I was dismissed. This upset me as I didn't understand why she didn't do something about it. Do something to stop him doing it to other children. The crack in my perception of 'Adults' emerged. Not easily deterred, I told my grandmother, in her laundry, with the old concrete tubs, the washing machine with rollers attached and the smell of soap. I'll never forget this moment because it shocked me. She told me there are things you don't talk about, and what had been done to me was one of them. The crack in my view of adults widened and deepened. Much to my Nan's irritation I kept talking about what the senior relative had done to me. I told the wrong people; it fell on deaf ears.

It has been my experience, both personal and observed, that a great many parents, and relatives, can be relied upon for one thing; to make life as easy as possible for themselves. It's easier to ignore unpleasant things, and, in many cases blame the Victim, than to do something to support the Victim. To hold the predator accountable takes courage.

One afternoon a man with the same name as the senior relative knocked on my Nan's door. Sent from God (Church) he was selling books. I loved books; however, I couldn't understand why God would have a man like that working for him. I wasn't from a religious family; however, I remember being totally horrified and angry with God, and told him so.

No matter your age, keep telling people, different people, eventually someone will listen. Don't give up! Things are different from when I was young. There are school counsellors, school pastors, and teachers are legally required to report concerns relating to child sexual assault to police. Please, if your child tells you someone has sexually assaulted them, regardless of who the sexual predator is, don't ignore them or you could lose them. Always remember they are traumitised and might not be able to tell you everything. Expect there is more. Don't downgrade the seriousness of what happened to them. Never be relieved if your child/ren seems to have forgotten about it. How to respond to your child being sexually assaulted should go in your plan.

As I discussed earlier, in primary school, the police came to talk to us about 'Stranger Danger' and 'Red Light and Green Light People'. We sat cross-legged, squashed into the school library and watched a video, trying to guess who was a 'Green Light', safe person, and who was a 'Red Light', unsafe person. The police didn't tell us why the 'Red Light' person was unsafe, but I knew it was because they were like the senior relative. I remember being shocked that the woman with the dog was a 'Red Light' person, and the man sitting on a park bench was a 'Green Light' person.

The police told us there was a 'Red Light' man driving around telling children that their mother was in the hospital, and that he had been sent to take them to the hospital. The police said if this happens say, "That's my mother there" and run and tell someone what happened and tell them to call the police. We were told not to get into the car.

I attended a country school, and walked to and from school, crossing the main road we lived on. To school I walked up the road, through an apple orchard, climbing across the fence into the neighbouring front paddock/driveway and through the back gate of my school. That afternoon walking home along Junction Road, between the orchard and my driveway, a man pulled up in his car. He said exactly what the police had said the 'Red Light' man would say. Like a good little robot, following my programming, I pointed to an oncoming car and said exactly what the police had told us to say. The man took off, gravel flying over me as he sped off.

I crossed the road, ran home, and told Mum about the police visit and what had just happened. Mum told me not to be silly and to stop making things up. The crack in my perception of adults grew. Don't dismiss your child. It is very upsetting. For me, who had a poor self-image, my mother's response was both infuriating and devastating.

Did my mother report the incident to police? I don't know. Did he manage to get a child into his car that afternoon? I don't know. That was the only time during my school years that anyone came to talk to students about sexual predators.

When I was around seven years old, our boarder came into my life. If not for him I'm not sure I'd still be here. Kindness costs nothing and his abundant kindness meant so much to me and helped me cope with the next monster.

In the dead of night, HE came for eight-year-old me. I remember hearing later our boarder had asked if he could bring his friend home to watch the All Blacks playing a test match televised at midnight, after a few beers at the pub.

My sleepy green eyes opened to a stranger's black hair, his mouth latched onto my tiny breast and his finger hurting my inside girl parts. As I awoke my mind registered, I was in my bed, it was dark, and this stranger was kissing me, touching my breast and hurting me inside; his heavy breathing and the stink of his excitement assaulted my senses. Lying on my bed paralysed, confused and scared, I woke fully.

Are you thinking scream, scream for help? Too late, I was in shock, my body had frozen, no words came from my mouth. It is impossible to think or behave rationally when your body goes into 'Freeze' and shock sets in. I stopped breathing. Are you thinking "Punch him, kick him, fight back"? Apparently, 'Fight' is not the most common reaction, 'Freeze' is. No, I didn't scream or fight, I was barely making sense of what was happening, when he spoke.

He said he was in the wrong room and asked where the bathroom was. Little scared eight-year-old me told him it was on the other side of the hallway to my bedroom. He left the room. Fully awake and fighting through the confusion, my heart stopped, fear seized me; I saw him peeking at me through the gap the hinges made between the door and the doorframe.

Smiling, he calmly came back into the room, asked where our boarder's room was. I told him to go outside the house, and at the side of the house is a shed, and our boarder's room is at the end of the shed. He told eight-year-old, terrified me, if I showed him where our boarder's room was, he would leave me alone. I really wanted him to leave me alone. I was terrified, the thought of him leaving me alone and not doing what the senior relative had done to me anymore consumed me. I agreed to show him.

Are you thinking I was 'stupid' or 'dumb'? No, I wasn't, I was a terrified eight-year-old who had just been sexually assaulted. Understand it's not the Victim's fault. If a paedophile or rapist has chosen you then you won't know until they strike, and don't expect to be able to save yourself; it's not that simple, at any age. It took me a long time to understand this. At the time, I was a terrified child in shock, and he was in control.

He followed me from my bedroom, turning left into the hallway. At the 'L' shaped corner, through the lounge door, I could see our boarder asleep on the floor. We walked through the poolroom and office, out onto the back porch where I stood pointing to the white door at the far end of the shed. When I looked back at him, I realized he was standing in the doorway, blocking my path to safety.

In the years following the senior relative's assault I'd openly, anywhere, anytime, asked my mother about sex. Finally, Mum had sat me down near her glass china cabinet and told me about sex. How the man puts his penis into the woman's vagina, how men want to do this with lots of women until they're in their twenties when they get married because they want someone to look after them. Standing there looking at him, it hit me, he wasn't going to let me go. He was going to put his penis inside me, and I didn't want him to do that. I ran screaming for my eight-year-old life. Although I was short, I could run, and I ran like a terrified rabbit, screaming "Help". Years later, my brother, then five years old, told me he remembered waking up and seeing me running away from a man, screaming. Despite him being a grown man, around 20 years of age, I ran around the house ten times before he caught me. Yes, I counted, ten times past the glass sliding doors of my parents' bedroom. He carried me over his shoulder, like a sack of potatoes, to our boarder's isolated bedroom.

He put me down in front of the single bed. He was standing in front of me smiling; he stank like the senior relative. I remember thinking, I know what he is going to do, and how I was going to get away. I stood in front of him, the bed at my back, his legs apart in an 'A' shape, while he undid his jeans. Fear of the unknown didn't block me; I waited for my moment to act. As he was pulling down his jeans, momentarily immobilised, I dove between his legs. That door always stuck, and it usually took me several pulls to open it, so I put one hand on the doorframe, and one on the door, and pulled for all I was worth. Miraculously it opened, and again I ran. I didn't look back. I could hear him right behind me. Slamming the glass sliding door and locking it, we came face to face.

Crying, I ran into the lounge and tried desperately to wake our boarder. Next thing I remember I was back in my bed crying and my parents were asking what was wrong. I told them. The police were called, and I remember hearing Dad wake up our boarder, tell him what had happened, and ask him to keep his friend in his room until the police arrived. The police arrived and I told them what had happened. I remember feeling embarrassed, sitting on the round wooden Chinese-carved coffee table with six small stools under it, answering questions as the policeman wrote in his black notebook. He asked me, "Do you want to get up in court and say what he did to you?" I said, "Yes." I waited and waited for my day in court; it didn't come.

When I was 52 my father told me he had gone to a meeting with the chief of the New Plymouth Police Department. Dad said he had been told that if the paedophile was prosecuted for what he had done to me, he would go to jail for about 10 years, and given that he had already been incarcerated for several years, it was thought that it would be too long a period of time for him to be locked up. Dad said the police chief explained the paedophile would serve out the rest of his original sentence, prior to being paroled, at a jail away from New Plymouth. When I heard this, I felt numb. Does this seem fair to you? Should the paedophile be more important than the child he abused?

In December 2018 over coffee and waffles Mum told me this predator was prosecuted, found guilty and ordered to pay me $140.00, which he still owes. New Plymouth Court has no record of this. Writing this, I'm 55 years old and don't know the outcome. Never do this to your children.

No-one from the New Plymouth Police Department, or any other social services department, spoke to me about what had happened; there was no counselling for me or my parents. Does it make sense to you I was forgotten about? If you ever hear someone say, "Why didn't she report it at the time?" maybe, like me, she/he did, and it fell on deaf ears. I've heard of many women reporting to police to be told it was: "He said she said" and they couldn't prosecute so they didn't investigate.

At the time, following this assault, I remember my mother being angry when I asked about when I would be going to court. She told me it hadn't happened, and to stop making things up. This lie damaged me and heightened the flashbacks; it was like it was happening 'right now'.

How family and friends react towards a loved one who has been sexually assaulted can make the trauma worse or help them access the correct, much-needed support. Make sure you know what support you should give.

Following this assault my parents ignored me. Our boarder talked to me. We played board games and laughed. I felt safe with him. He left us several months after the assault and I've always been grateful for having had him in my life.

I was young, not stupid; I saw my parent's denial as the ultimate betrayal, because I knew it had happened. I lived with the relentless daily flashbacks and memories seeped into my nightmares. Night after night I woke, lying still, too scared to move, silently gasping for breath. Betrayal twice in a few years, this was devastating. I remember going into shock again, being hit with a blast of numbness, the horror of another betrayal so painful, I truly died inside.

Burying himself in the newspaper was my father's escape, gardening was my mother's. I had no escape. I remember slapping at the newspaper, screaming my pain at my father, arguing with my mother about what had happened, resulting in beltings. Apparently, I was a very naughty child. Slicing jug cords and cutting up belts was my protection. Then a relative, who never hit her children, suggested she was planning on using a weeping willow twig. We had a weeping willow. I couldn't chop down a whole tree. Corporal punishment bred resentment and the cycle continued. If not for our boarder, my perception of men could have been very negative. I remember during general social conversation my father said, "Anyone lay a hand on my kids I'd kill them." "Liar," I thought: "What a coward, so weak … didn't do that for me."

My formal education went downhill, because the flashbacks assaulted me day and night. I didn't trust anyone, and I lost the ability to form healthy friendships, compromising myself and feeding my self-loathing. I was trapped in victim mode, incorporating defensive behaviour into my daily interactions, making me unpopular and disliked. I remember being dragged to a birthday party for one of the girls from primary school. I hadn't wanted to go, and as expected I was bullied. I sat there numb and alone until the end of the party, because the girl's mother didn't want to call Mum to come get me. She told me I was imagining things. My fault again. During my primary school years one of my teachers relentlessly bullied me and although there was the option to move schools I was left trapped in his class.

I've heard people say it doesn't matter what happens to you in childhood, that's the past. They've said you shouldn't blame your childhood for your problems, sort yourself out. Do you share these sentiments? On reflection, do you think such statements are valid? To me, it's another way for people to blame the Victim, rather than accept the reality of sexual assault trauma and be more understanding of Victims.

I know what the senior relative did to me and I knew what 'HE' did. Telling me it didn't happen was a big mistake; it cost my parents their daughter, and destined me to a long, dysfunctional life as a Victim. Don't make the mistake of thinking children forget; I didn't, and I know of others who didn't forget.

When my mother said it was all in my imagination, my whole world disintegrated. In my mind, there was a cover-up and my parents were part of it. To me, that made no sense, they were supposed to protect me. I resented them with every fibre of my being. Their betrayal consumed me. It wasn't a good time for any of us. Each person deals with events in life differently, and the wishes of the Victim should be respected and supported, regardless of how inconvenient or uncomfortable it is for others.

As a mum there have been times when I've wanted to formally complain or charge certain teachers for their bad behaviour (not sexual assault) towards my daughter. However, I chose to listen to what my daughter wanted, or needed, over what I wanted. It happened to her, not me. Instead, I focused on helping her to survive what had happened, in a constructive way to prevent her becoming vulnerable.

In my 20s, I was having a social coffee within a group when an upset mum told us her daughter had been 'interfered with'. She wanted to take her young teenage daughter to the police to report the incident. Her daughter didn't want to do this. The group shared mixed opinions. I told them all that I knew what I was talking about first-hand, and that my wishes weren't respected. I told this mum she had no right to pressure her daughter. Her job was to respect her daughter's wishes and to get her counselling. I warned she could lose her daughter if she didn't support her. In my opinion, it can be very scary for a parent or friend, but the Victim's needs and decisions must be respected. Do you agree with my advice? Why/Why not?

As a child with a strong sense of social justice, being on the receiving end of two cover-ups wasn't healthy. At 14 years old, all that resentment, hurt and pain spewed out of me as I screamed at my mother one afternoon, reducing her to tears. Her defence about the second child sexual assault: "I was only doing what the police told me to do. They said you'd forget about it." Confirmation of betrayal, this fuelled such rage in me. Firstly, my mother didn't fight for me; instead, she tried to bury what happened. Then the police, the people who were supposed to protect the innocent, had instigated the cover-up. No-one has the right to decide what is right for a Victim except the Victim. Eight-year-old me had told that policeman I wanted to go to court. Adding insult to injury my mother then claimed she hadn't done anything about the senior relative assaulting me because she "couldn't go against her family". I think what she meant was she couldn't go against her mother.

To me, when Mum said those words, she made the senior relative more important than me. I was totally, emotionally destroyed. When I was sexually assaulted, I was stripped of my identity; looking in the mirror I didn't recognise the little girl, nor did I understand this experience. Left to my own inadequate devices to put myself back together, bitterness, fear, self-loathing and resentment were sadly the key ingredients. I punished my mother, saying if protecting me was going against her family, then who was I? I must have been adopted. Relentlessly I repeatedly asked who my real family were. Where did I come from? Why had she adopted me if she didn't want me?

What I didn't realise then was people cope differently. They're only capable of dealing with what they can cope with. Mum did what she could cope with and thought best. My parents weren't trained or educated about helping their children deal with sexual assault. What happened to me was very upsetting for them. They did the best they could. In my experience my parents' response is typical. Even today parents ignore or respond ineffectively when dreadful things are done to their children, and often blame their children. As parents, we must look at our own issues around sexual assault and get help if needed to ensure we react constructively to our chidren.

If you think you've been betrayed don't be like me, don't waste your life trapped in Victim mode. Please, find someone who will listen, because if you don't, you will be a Victim. Find the help, be brave, do the work and take care of yourself and be a Survivor.

Looking back, I lacked a sense of security, trusted no-one, felt no-one loved me and believed I was totally alone, trapped in a loveless family. I was dysfunctional, existing in a permanent state of fear, pain, anger and confusion. It made me desperate for approval, which in turn made me vulnerable, the perfect prey; or did it?

To this day I can remember my 12-year-old excitement when I found my cousin was coming to stay while her parents were away. Given my lack of self-respect, I felt so special our home had been chosen. We had a lot of fun, and to my mother's horror, against my aunt's wishes, I pierced my cousin's ears with a darning needle and a lot of ice. We got sick and Mum took us to the medical centre, waiting for us in the car. As our GP was away, I saw a fill-in doctor, who calmly, with authority, told me to take off my underpants and lie on the bed. I told him I had a sore throat and ears and I wasn't sore down there. We argued; he tried to convince me that he had to examine my vagina to diagnose my throat and ears. Finally, he looked at my throat and ears, whilst I remained upright and fully clothed. Mum told me I'd imagined it. I know better, and over the years have wondered how many lives that doctor destroyed?

Other than my love of reading, my education continued to falter as I never managed to overcome the effects of the sexual assaults, or the reactions of those meant to protect me. We were learning basic fractions and percentages around the time of the second sexual assault and to this day, I have anxiety attacks around math.

Friendships were shaky. I remember one afternoon I was out riding my pony with girls from my class, when we had a falling out. I don't remember why. As they rode off, my pony, Dusky Star, put his front hoof through the reins, and I panicked. I cried, calling for help. They laughed and said to unbuckle the reins. I can remember the overwhelming fear of being alone, coupled with an intense feeling of self-loathing at being so needy. I considered myself truly pathetic.

Mum tried to help me, first buying my pony, which we absolutely couldn't afford. She sent me off to Brownies. I didn't want to go. I made it clear to everyone I didn't want to be there. I felt exposed; everyone was so nice to me. I thought this was because they'd been told I was a problem child. I went through the motions without forming any friendships. Now I can appreciate their efforts.

Teenage Years ...

At New Plymouth Girls High School initiation day, I met my first friend for life, and although our roads have been bumpy, we've kept in touch and remained close. Her friendship has been invaluable.

This friend babysat up the road from my aunt. One night, when I was sleeping over with my cousins, we went up to see her. Some male friends dropped in. One of them had paid me a bit of attention in the past. Desperate dumb teenager, I didn't realise he'd been grooming me. He planned to have sex with 15-year-old me. He came prepared with a bag of white pills. My friend caught him preparing my cocktail. New rules: I opened my drinks, I filled my cup and as I ventured into pubs, I never left a drink unattended and returned to drink it. For the most part my friends and I bought our own drinks. At a party we left what we were drinking in our car, and guarded our keys with our lives, because if you don't, it could cost you your life. Please, in teenage years and early twenties you don't see yourselves as the perfect prey, but to the practised predator you are. No, I never told adults what he'd tried to do.

Although studying wasn't going well for me, second year high school I wrote a piece my English teacher was very excited about. To my absolute horror, my lovely, inspired, kind teacher read it to the class. To encourage me, I had to read it out in form assembly. Totally exposed and panicked, I vowed never to make this mistake again. I wanted to achieve, wanted to go to university, I wanted to become a vet. I buried ability and dashed my dreams. Don't say "you could've tried harder" or "it's just an excuse" unless you've walked in my shoes.

Since the screaming match I had with my mother, I had planned my escape from a house where I believed I wasn't wanted. Hopeful one year of night school hairdressing would get me a job, there were no apprenticeships when I started looking. The day I turned 16, having secured a job, I left home, taking the pain with me. I moved into a rental with a girl I knew from school. Big mistake. Our friendship was based on a mutual understanding of emotional pain. Damaged, dysfunctional people attract other damaged, dysfunctional people and abusers. The friendship fell apart and I moved in with a male, platonic friend. I thought living with a man would keep me safe. You might be thinking, what an idiot. Is what happened next my fault? Could I have foreseen it?

I love water and late one weekend afternoon I'd been reading in the bath; wrapped in a towel I returned to my bedroom to dry off. It happened so quickly I don't think I had time to blink. He walked in right behind me. I didn't know his name. I'd seen him around on a few occasions. I didn't realise he was there until he grabbed me; next thing I knew, before my mind had time to realise what was happening, he'd flung me on the bed, his pants were down, and he was on top of me so fast the shock momentarily immobilised me. Imagine how practised he would have to be to put all those separate moves together into one smooth, swift movement. The timing was spot on. He came prepared, I don't remember him wearing underpants.

With his weight bearing down on me I struggled to free my hands, pinned above my head. Screaming for help, I kept moving my body in tiny movements to prevent his erect penis, already slamming up against me, from penetrating me. He was smiling as he pushed his finger inside me, the weight of his body trapping me. I was outmatched in muscle, strength and stamina. Again, he tried to push his penis inside me, it was in just past the entrance; as he thrust, I tilted, his penis hit the side of my vagina and was out. Smiling, again and again he forced himself into me, without full penetration. I think he raped me with his finger several more times during our struggle.

After what seemed like forever, I was exhausted, my strength was failing me; however, all my screaming saved me. This man was visiting my flatmate with friends. I don't know who took pity on me and rescued me. I heard a knocking on the front door and someone said they were my father and wanted to see me. I knew it wasn't my father. The rapist stopped. He got up, pulled up his jeans and left.

Later my flatmate claimed the rapist had told the group I'd been asking for it, flirting with him, I wanted him. It wasn't my flatmate who rescued me. One of the other men obviously felt uncomfortable, realising what the rapist said wasn't true, and stopped the assault. I moved out, going to live with my grandparents. I was covered in bruises around my wrists, inside my thighs and there was a slight bleeding from my damaged insides. I remember it stung to go to the toilet for a week.

Imagine you're sitting in a jury, you've read what he'd be claiming, you've read my account of this rape, who would you blame? Would you convict a young working man, in his early twenties, with no criminal record? Or would you blame the young girl for causing it because she was flatting with a male flatmate? If I hadn't been rescued, and the rape had continued, too tired to fight back, would you have considered my not continuing to fight back as consent? Would you find this man not guilty? Alternatively, if I'd stayed in 'Freeze' mode instead of going into 'Fight' mode, and not screamed or fought, would you convict him? What if his lawyers put me on trial, accusing me of flirting with his client at various times, accusing me of being responsible because I hadn't installed a lock on my rental bedroom door? Would you accept his 'not guilty' plea or believe me and convict? In my opinion, not convicting sends two messages: One telling the Victim they're worthless, and the other to predators suggesting this 'story' is a good line of defence to rely on in future.

At my grandparents, I experienced a window of peace. I started running again and feeling stronger. The calm before the storm.

One Saturday night, my girlfriend and I met up with a few male friends at a dance, held in the New Plymouth Courthouse Hall. There was a man there I hadn't met before, whose name I don't remember. Even though we all hung out as a group, harmlessly dancing the night away, he kept trying to isolate me. I kept as far away from him as I could.

After the dance we went back to the home of one of the men in our group. He lived not far from my grandparents. We watched *The Young Ones* and ate fish and chips. Everyone was going to stay on and watch sports, and I wanted to go home. Saying goodbye, I intended to walk the 10-minute stroll home. The stranger offered me a lift, which I graciously declined. Not the response he'd planned. Not giving up, he solicited everyone else's support to get me into his car. I said I didn't know him and that I was happy to walk home. Everyone insisted I'd be safer with a lift home, vouching for their friend, this wolf in sheep's clothing. Against my better judgement, I got into the front passenger-side bucket seat of his car.

Having run red lights, stop signs and give ways, he stopped at a remote section of the New Plymouth coastline. I don't remember where, I was too busy screaming, and panicking, with shock setting in.

The car stopped. As I was about to escape out the open passenger door, he expertly grabbed me, forcibly jamming me between the front car seats, my head dangling in the air, with no neck support. I was trapped. He was on me, his penis hard against the outside of my vagina, his mouth sucking at my neck and breasts. He repeatedly panted: "You want me." I struggled, screaming, "This is rape." With his finger thrusting inside me I screamed, "This is rape." As he thrust his erection at me over and over again, I kept screaming, "Stop … this is rape", moving my bottom so he kept missing my vagina. He got frustrated, restricted my meagre ability to move and managed to gain partial entry inside me still panting, "You want me." Screaming, "This is rape," I tilted my body and he smacked into my inside wall, more struggled movement and he was out. This continued while he repeated, "You want me." I screamed, "I don't want you; this is rape." I don't know how long I struggled and screamed, "This is rape" and "I don't want you." I don't know why he stopped, calmly yanked me out from between the bucket seats, put on his seatbelt and drove me home. Shocked, shaking and exhausted I could barely breathe. I couldn't think straight. I couldn't move. He stopped outside my grandparents' home. I got out of the car. He drove off saying nothing. I remember standing on the footpath; I don't remember going inside the house; I remember being in my bed.

Sunday, another family gathering for tea. I was in the bath, stiff and sore, aching all over, suck marks covering my neck and torso with savage bruising on my inner thighs, soaking my swollen genitals, when Mum burst in yelling at me, calling me a slut. I told her what had happened, only to be told apparently an older cousin had decided I'd willingly chosen to have consensual sex, and later regretted it, or not wanting to be thought of badly, had cried "Rape". I don't know if one of my cousins said this; however, instead of checking, I accepted my mother's version, and for many years I held resentment towards my cousin. If this situation occurred today, I would speak with my cousin. Instead, dysfunctional, broken, battered, bruised, shocked me with tears rolling down my face, yet again a disappointment to my family, hid and festered. I had no fight left. I was dead and this marked the beginning of dysfunctionally rebuilding my identity. This incident with Mum being the early building blocks.

I told my girlfriend about the assault and she spoke to the other men in the group, who had vouched for their friend. They asked my friend to take me up to the Westown Hotel, Friday night. They asked me what happened, and I told them. During the evening I heard from someone, I don't remember who, he'd been sorted. During the evening five girls around my age came up to me, individually. They thanked me for speaking out. They shared with me that as he panted the words "You want me" he had raped them. I was the first person to speak out, and have often wondered how many more teenage girls he had sentenced to the realm of the Living Dead? This was the first time in my life as a Victim that I didn't feel alone, and I was supported. This meant a lot to me. If his friends hadn't vouched for him, would their response have been different? As a jury member, without the support of these men vouching for him, would you find him guilty? He said, she said. Would you believe the bruising was consensual, rough sex?

Not long after this sexual assault I got a call from my mother, at work, telling me my belongings were on the footpath. My grandmother no longer wanted me living there. I was told not to go in and talk to my grandmother. Through her kitchen window my grandmother watched me walk away homeless with my suitcase in hand. My friend's mother took me in.

About two weeks before his death, Gramps met me at the bus stop, on my way home from work. He told me he was going to die soon. He wanted me to know that my family didn't understand what I'd been through and asked me to forgive them. Although I didn't really understand at the time, he was trying to help me understand if people haven't experienced something, are in denial about an experience or haven't been educated about it, then they can't understand, accept it or deal with it. I've run many research discussions on this topic over the years. One of the reasons I'm writing this book is to give you insight.

Disaster struck on February 10, 1983. I was at work listening to the radio when the report came on. There had been a fatality at a house fire and several other people were taken to hospital. The phone rang. I was told Gramps was dead, murdered. My family was gathering at Nan's. There were hugs and tears. Over the time I stayed with my grandparents, Gramps had been a source of great compassion and support. Now he was gone. A lost, lonely, devastated, scarred teenager sat outside the courthouse during the trial, but couldn't go in. The murderer was jailed for 10 years.

People come and go in the periphery of groups. There was a man in his 20s who started turning up more and more at parties I attended. He forced himself into my immediate space, sitting right next to me, standing on top of me, following me to the toilet and bailing me up against walls. I repeatedly told him to leave me alone, but he wouldn't. Roger, my friend's brother's dog, chased him off, baring his teeth. When Roger wasn't around, I hid, hung in big groups with lots of men, or snuck out and went home. One night at a party I was tired, it was late, and I had a two-hour walk home. Choosing to wait for a lift, I locked the door of my friend's bedroom, and went to sleep. He was found trying to force the external bedroom window open while I slept. Whose fault do you think it would have been if he'd got in and raped me? As a jury member would you consider I asked for it because I went to sleep, after locking the door. Would you blame me because I stayed, knowing he was there? Would you believe I'd decided to open the window and let him in? Or, with his mum crying in the back of the court, would you hold this young man, dressed nicely in a new suit, with his life ahead of him, responsible for his actions?

About a year after Gramp's death I returned home to live. I attended New Plymouth Polytechnic studying Office Studies, including typing, shorthand and bookkeeping, and went to work at the Taranaki Museum. I loved my time there working with wonderful, decent, caring people. I loved history, so I found my environment fascinating. During my employment I ended up hanging off a fence after a drunk driver slammed into the motorbike I was getting a lift home on. After months in hospital, I spent months in a plaster attempting to stimulate delayed bone growth, possibly due to unnecessary dieting. After the plaster came off, I successfully begged my treating physician to perform a forced manipulation under anaesthetic to get movement back. Following months of painful physiotherapy, I almost have full range of movement. I drew on resilience and determination to overcome my obstacles and recover. Acknowledging your achievements and strengths is important.

At parties, I was usually the girl in the corner, an observer learning, taking notes. I didn't I know I was being watched.

Following an Icehouse concert in Palmerston North, about a three-hour drive from my hometown, New Plymouth, we went on to a party. Perched in a corner a man I'd never met started talking to me. He proceeded to describe his favourite outfits in my wardrobe and when I'd worn them. I knew stalkers are dangerous as someone stalking a family member was convicted of murdering my grandfather. Now I was confronted with the fact that I had a stalker. This really shook me because I had no idea I was being stalked. You don't know what other people are thinking. Be aware, be alert, stick with your friends and don't write yourself off with booze or drugs; it won't be your fault if anything happens, but it could be fatal.

Twenties ...

Breakups can be difficult, and some occasions can become dangerous, when one or the other party doesn't want to let go. I had an ex-boyfriend stalker. He followed me, searched for me, stood in front of me on the dance floors of various establishments, staring at me. He visited my friends. He'd turn up at places he shouldn't. On one of these occasions I was so upset I drank. Later I was found in a ditch, torn clothes, badly bruised with swollen genitals, hysterically babbling my ex had raped me. On waking in my bed, the next morning, I had little memory of this. I don't know the full details of what happened;

however, I have physical sickening flashbacks with a sense of violence, me struggling and feeling terrified unable to breathe. Please, take stalking seriously.

My arrival in Sydney ended my struggle with bulimia. I was back in the gym and I enrolled in a self-development deportment class with a former Miss Australia, transforming my self-image. This wonderful woman, and friend over the years, encouraged me to take acting lessons and here I thrived. Acting is about 'Truth' and truth was my friend. Truth was the one thing which never let me down. Sundays were special, I loved my drama classes. My girlfriend from New Plymouth came to Sydney to complete a Palliative Care course, on the eve of class embarking on a section of work involving self-exploration through masks. We were tasked with making a mask representative of ourselves. This dearest friend gave me a great gift, an insight into another side of me she saw that I didn't know existed. My friend said she saw me as a love heart covered in pink silk with lots of glitter and sparkles. A totally alien image to me. I trusted her and together we shopped. I constructed the mask, surprising myself. My friend and mask classes gave me back a side of myself I'd lost. I believe it was a significant turning point towards internal self-analysis. Although the road ahead was bumpy and the light at the end of the tunnel was a pinprick, at least it was there.

Competition can be intense, and to succeed it requires sacrifice. There were a limited number of places in a specific drama class I really wanted to get accepted into. The audition required we share something personal. We needed to demonstrate we could 'risk'. We had to show something which stood us apart from everyone else. Standing in front of strangers, with a few faces I knew, alone, I risked everything. For the first time I publicly shared my sexual assault story. I felt exposed, numb, naked, laid out bare. Speaking my story out loud to strangers was a huge step forward for me because I acknowledged the assaults, my pain and dysfunction. Owning my own truth gained me entry into the course and supported my transformation.

At the conclusion of a relationship which needed to end, I joined a dating agency, expensive in those days, to find out what I wanted in a partner. Although I met a lot of men, I dated one. He is such a lovely man, and I don't know what he did to deserve dysfunctional me. Nearing the end of our time together he shared with me his visit to a gifted tarot card reader, who told him I wasn't the one, explaining there was a lovely lady for him. I hope he found this lucky lady and they're both very happy. Over the years I went to see this tarot card reader several times which was a good decision.

As a victim I had an unhealthy, deep-seated need to please, which I wasn't aware of. This meant I failed to stand up for myself and be heard, leading to a permanent pain-related disability. I found a workplace where I felt at home. However, my commitment to an acting career saw me turn down a permanent position. The girl they employed for the position wasn't working out and I accepted permanent employment with them. The plan was to let her go once she finished her trial period. I was temporarily moved to an unsatisfactory working environment. My complaints about the unergonomic workstation causing me physical symptoms were acknowledged and I was promised it would be addressed. It wasn't. I remember a doctor I was seeing told me not to tell anyone what was happening and to hide it. He explained no-one wanted to know about it. I was really scared. My treating chiropractor, having taken a lot of money from me, having told me not to be concerned, eventually told me there was nothing more he could do. I couldn't work, I couldn't feed myself, struggled to get dressed and was in horrendous pain. Regardless, I was determined to recover, like I had in the past.

This work-related injury resulted in me sitting in the long, dark corridor of the Kent Street Work Cover office. It was here another angel appeared before me, in the form of a middle-aged lady. This angel asked me if I'd seen any insurance doctors. I hadn't. She generously warned me about a monster, sharing her story of sexual abuse. My angel told me to be very careful if I went to see Dr #, telling me how he positions the chair he wants clients to sit in at a certain distance from his desk, allowing him free movement. She told me he had stood behind her and reached down to fondle her breast. Then moved in front of her, pulling her head towards him, forcing his penis into her mouth. This kind, brave lady shared she wasn't the only one. The referral letter sending me for an assessment with Dr # was waiting for me when I got home. She saved me, because I had time to think. I decided he wasn't thrusting his erection into my mouth without whatever fight I could manage with my limited physical ability.

On entering his room, I pushed the chair forward, sitting down, squashed up against his desk. Displeased, he proceeded to ask me questions, telling me I had a permanent, pain-related injury and would never return to my job or do that type of work again. He told me I probably wouldn't work again.

Time for his examination. He told me to "Get up". He moved the chair back to its original position, and walking around to the back of the chair, he told me to "Sit". Sitting, I crossed my arms over my breasts and bent down as his left hand slid from my shoulder, forcing its way under my arms and cupping my breast. After barking at me to sit up, he said obviously I wasn't as bad as I was making out because I could use my arms.

As I sat up and he moved around in front of me, his right hand, which had been resting on my right shoulder, travelled up my neck, anchoring at the back of my head. His zip was down. Before he could make his next move, I told him I knew what he was going to do, and if he put "that anywhere near me, I'd bite it off". Rage swept over him; fly down, he turned as red as a tomato. He reminded me of a big, red, nasty, festering pimple under so much pressure it was about to burst.

He stormed to the door, opened it and screamed at me, "Get out" in front of a confused waiting room full of people. I left. The police told me it was an insurance matter. I later found out Dr #'s behaviour was well known throughout the medico-legal world, and despite this knowledge, nothing was done to stop him.

Next, I was sent to another insurance doctor, Dr Safe. On entering his room, standing near the door, I asked if he was going to try what Dr # had tried. Dr Safe told me he was aware of what Dr # did to women and assured me he was nothing like Dr #. He said he got paid to say whatever the insurer wanted; however, he refused to hurt people. Doctor Safe told me I had sustained a permanent injury and would probably never return to permanent full-time work, explaining a return-to-work program would be a waste of time.

A very inexperienced, uncomfortable Dr Rescue made a very clumsy attempt to be sexually inappropriate with me. I call him Dr Rescue because I rescued him. It was clear to me he was uncomfortable about sexually assaulting me. I confronted him about his attempt, and an embarrassed, apologetic Dr Rescue agreed to a return-to-work program while telling me it wouldn't work. It failed.

From that point, other than Dr Safe, I refused to see an insurance doctor without another person in the room. I was thrown out of doctors' offices; they didn't want the extra company, not even if it was their nurse or secretary. No, there was no big payout, that's a fallacy.

Do you think Dr #'s attempted oral penetration was a crime? Despite having escaped the oral sexual assault I was warned about, I experienced extreme distress. Leaving Dr #'s surgery, shaken, I realised I was being followed. At home I was terrified of what the insurance investigators were going to do to me. I'd heard stories about their tactics from other patients in Workcover and went on to hear many dreadful stories in insurance doctors' waiting rooms.

During this time in my life my self-awareness journey flourished, using the various techniques I've already mentioned to break my dysfunctional subconscious behavioural patterns. This work was a journey into self, supported with research, study and professional counselling, which included developing formal skill sets for dealing with anxiety and panic attacks, and building self-trust. During this time, I also supported others in their journey, which is something I've continued to do on an informal basis.

After a period my disability stabilised and I learnt how to manage it, never using pain medication. I took a media workshop enabling me to become employed with *A Current Affair* for about 12 months. I enjoyed my work until my disability made it impossible to continue, despite the boxes of anti-inflammatory medication I was chewing like there was no tomorrow. I hate to think of what my determination to be able to support myself did to my poor tummy.

Despondent, I saw the tarot card reader again. She is a lovely lady. Sadly, she didn't have good news for me. As kindly as possible she told me that a very bad thing was going to happen to me. She told me she was very sorry that I had to go through this bad thing, after everything else I'd been through. She told me she couldn't say what it was that was going to happen, just that it was very, very bad. Then she told me it was really important not to focus on what was going to happen when it happened. Instead, she told me to focus on surviving, using the analogy of a train that had been derailed, and now it was time for me to put myself back on track. This was invaluable advice and following a very bad thing I latched onto it.

Taking Back My Power ...

May 1996, horrendous pain woke me. Mr Pleaded Guilty, my friend's husband, was forcing his erect penis inside me, from behind, with his arms wrapped around me to help him enter me. His young son not a metre away, asleep in another bed. His wife, my friend, asleep in her room. I have included my police statements, my witness statement and my Victim Impact Statement, formally produced through the Royal North Shore Hospital Sexual Assault Unit, on my website. I've chosen to do this to give you a formalised insight into what sexual assault is, and the effect it has on Victims.

I'd known Mr Pleaded Guilty and his wife for many years. I'd celebrated the birth of their two beautiful, healthy babies, and supported them through a rough patch, supposedly due to his drinking. Mr Pleaded Guilty's wife and the children stayed in my rental for a few months after I moved in with my long-time boyfriend, this relationship ending prior to the sexual assault.

Mr Pleaded Guilty's wife had hosted a lingerie party, and Mr Pleaded Guilty had gone out with friends. The plan was I'd stay over and go shopping with Mr Pleaded Guilty's wife and the children the next day.

The shock and horror of Mr Pleaded Guilty, a friend, sexually assaulting me was a struggle to comprehend. Stupidly, I had a shower. I'm an Aquarian water-baby. When I'm upset getting into a bath or shower is an automatic response for me. It's also where I often do my best thinking. You should put in your plan DON'T have a shower. Go straight to the hospital so DNA can be collected.

Distressed, I left the house and got as far as the first phone box. I called my dear friend. I've been so lucky in my life to have such special friends. My dear friend is a lovely, calm, organised, common-sense person who got me moving. I drove to her place, just around the corner. From there she drove me to Westmead Hospital. She had phoned her friend, a policeman, who organised a specialist sexual assault IRAC police officer for me.

Although the swabs to test for DNA and test for possible sexually transmitted infections and AIDS were invasive, I was in good hands. I remember my legs, parted for the swabs, uncontrollably shaking and the tears streaming down my face were mopped up. My lovely nurses, and my dear friend, talked me through everything, held my hand and made me feel safe. Their voices soothed me, although I couldn't stop shaking. They cocooned me in warm blankets, isolated me, and never left me alone. They knew what to do, thought of everything, including the morning after pill. Although I was already on the pill, better safe than sorry. I began to feel safe and therefore I advocate medical care before law and order.

I knew I wanted to press charges, so I answered "Yes" when the police asked. I recommend every sexual assault victim make a police statement while everything is fresh in your mind. However, please understand it is typical to forget things, given the state a victim is in following an assault. You can write down things you later remember and make another statement. I found getting the experience out and on paper was a relief. I recommend when you call for an ambulance, stay on the line until it arrives. During this time tell the operator everything you can. It's being recorded and it's as close to Ground Zero, time of the actual assault, as possible. Alternatively record an account on your phone if you can think to do this.

You can decide later if you want to continue with your complaint. The court system provides a lot of opportunities for victims to decide not to proceed to trial. My advice is to make your statement/s, as I know, first-hand, it will help you. After you've been sexually assaulted you need to make everything about your transformation from being a Victim to a Survivor. The order part of law and order, the court system, is all about the predator's rights; however, don't let this dissuade you from going to court. For myself, and others I've spoken to, holding the predator accountable for what they did to us was very empowering, regardless of the outcome. It helped me transform into a Survivor.

The tarot card reader's words, ringing loudly in my ears, comforted me. I knew what direction I needed to focus. I focused on me, what I wanted, and how I wanted to get there. Before leaving Westmead's safe bosom, I was referred to the safe, caring, reassuring, knowledgeable walls of the Royal North Shore Hospital's Sexual Assault Unit, and Susan's team. As discussed, it was here, I put my life back on track, and again rebuilt myself as a Survivor.

After leaving Westmead Hospital, sitting in my dear friend's lounge, grateful for having such a beautiful friend, realisation hit me. I knew

I wasn't the only one. I also knew this wasn't his first attempt to sexually assault me.

A few months earlier Mr Pleaded Guilty's wife had contacted me, asking if I would come out to her place while she and the children were away visiting her parents, and have dinner with Mr Pleaded Guilty. She was asking because he had her believing he wouldn't cope with being alone the whole time she was away. She was worried about him. I agreed, and after finishing work at *ACA*, I made my way out to their Auburn rental. Mr Pleaded Guilty had cooked dinner; I don't remember what. He had uncorked the wine, ready to go. I declined the wine, saying I had to work the next day. He suggested I stay overnight in the spare bed. I ate my dinner, Mr Pleaded Guilty sitting in the middle of the couch and me sitting on the arm of the couch, with my feet on the couch so I could face him. We ate and chatted, then I went home. Nothing in his behaviour caused me alarm. He was his usual relaxed, friendly self, thanking me for coming, saying he was appreciative of my company.

A few days after Mr Pleaded Guilty assaulted me, his wife invited me over to their home saying Mr Pleaded Guilty wanted to apologise and explain his actions. I notified my police contact who warned me against going; however, I went. In their tiny kitchen, in front of his wife, a sobbing Mr Pleaded Guilty gave me a card apologising for what he'd done. Mr Pleaded Guilty was going out that night and after changing, when his wife had left the lounge where I was sitting, at the door he told me how he'd played with me and fondled my breast while I didn't know he was doing it. He relished each word, as he described assaulting me. He smiled while describing in detail the time he'd spent with me before I awoke.

After the assault, his wife shared with me that she often woke up to find him having sex with her while she was asleep. She said he told her she was so sexy or beautiful he couldn't help himself or thought she was awake. She also shared her concerns about a time while they were living in an ex-brothel rental. Mr Pleaded Guilty held parties at home for his sales team. After these parties, according to his wife, Mr Pleaded Guilty's female sales staff members would leave. This suggested to me there were a lot of women out there who he had assaulted.

The next day I made another statement to police placing his card, apologising for what he'd done to me, into evidence.

Mr Pleaded Guilty was charged with sexually assaulting me. Initially he didn't enter a plea. On the day of the trial, on the steps of the Parramatta Court, with another of his victims present to witness him being held accountable, I was told he pleaded guilty.

At the 1997 sentencing of Mr Pleaded Guilty, I set a legal precedent establishing the amount of suffering a Victim of sexual assault experiences. However, this precedent is based on my experience. Remember in the past I'd worked hard to resolve prior trauma and had a very clear focus supported with over 12 months of specialist counselling. If you're a judge, jury member, support person, or friend, please remember most sexual assault Victims don't have a similar foundation to fall back on. Therefore, make allowances for far worse trauma effects than I experienced.

A few weeks after the 1997 sentencing I received a call from the policeman shadowing my case. He was a very angry man. Apparently, someone had contacted Mr Pleaded Guilty's full-time employer. Further, according to the policeman, someone had contacted the employer for his part-time job managing a take-away pizza outlet at night. Despite there being no evidence identifying who had made the calls, the angry policeman had decided I somehow knew about this part-time job Mr Pleaded Guilty had secured since the sexual assault. He accused me of making the calls. He threatened to lock me up if any further calls were made.

About a year later, after Mr Pleaded Guilty's weekend jail sentence finished, I received ongoing disturbing phone calls, the male caller heavy breathing into the phone, which sounded to me sexual in nature, on my unlisted number. I called and reported the phone calls to police, including dates, times and durations. Police told me they were satisfied it was Mr Pleaded Guilty making the phone calls. They told me not to worry as he had pleaded guilty, meaning he was sorry for what he'd done, and it was unlikely he would act on the phone calls. They didn't consider I was in any danger; therefore, they wouldn't use their budget to trace the calls. No, they wouldn't ring and tell him to stop calling me as they didn't have any evidence it was him.

To me, the police appeared to be more concerned for the predator's wellbeing than the Victim's safety and well-being. Further, they didn't know who was calling me for months on end.

The Ever-Present Threat – Mindset Matters ...

In 2010, after my family moved from Singapore to the Philippines for my husband's work, my Survivor foundation was put to the test when I found myself in another threatening situation.

As mentioned, we moved into the Ayala Alabang community where I joined a Ladies group. This group's 2010 Halloween party was the first social evening my husband and I attended together. The party, held in someone's home, was a lavish catered affair with music and a bar. Like everyone we dressed up. I wore a little black 'V' bottomed dress, with feathers and beads, reaching just below the knee and a black pointy hat with purple strands. With my husband on my arm I was enjoying myself chatting to people until I went in search of a toilet.

In Philippine masions, where ex-pats live, every bedroom has an ensuite, there's a lobby ensuite and the study usually located downstairs has an ensuite. The lobby ensuite was occupied so one of the helpers directed me to the study. I locked the ensuite door.

Having seated myself on the toilet, I was startled; someone was shaking the door trying to open it. I was calling out "I'm in here … there's someone in here" as the door kept jiggling. The door opened. I stood up as an uninvited man walked into the rectangular space and turned to face me. Silently he began smiling. I knew he wasn't drunk; he hadn't been there very long. I don't drink and pay attention to what's going on around me. I was trapped in the loo, with my frillies around my shelltoes. I knew why he was standing there, staring at me, still silently smiling, glassy-eyed and reeking of that vile stench my nostrils know so well.

I resigned myself to being raped. I said: "Get out." He didn't move. No-one would hear me cry help. I wasn't afraid, I didn't go into shock, I didn't 'Freeze'. In Survivor mode, I smiled, saying there would be lots of blood, and evidence, people will know I didn't want it. Standing hands on hips, I said, "If you're going to do it, let's have at it."

He quietly stood there, looking at me. His smile faded, and he turned and left. A wise decision. I wasn't the Victim he was expecting. I didn't exhibit the behaviour he was used to. I was empowered with the knowledge I would survive, I had a plan and intended to fight and collect evidence.

My plan was to arm myself. I was going to rip the towel rail off the wall, break the mirror with the soap dispenser, wrap the hand towel around my hand to protect it, and using a shard of glass, my teeth and nails I'd tear him to bits while collecting as much DNA as possible. I intended to leave evidence of rape. People would know I wasn't a willing participant.

To me, he seemed very practised in his moves. I told my husband, who wanted to knock his head off. I said, "No." I didn't make a complaint because I couldn't prove anything; after all, what had he done? Accidentally opened a locked door and then left. We sat there watching him concoct his alibi. He loudly attracted attention, pretending to be reasonably tipsy, he proceeded to get publicly drunk.

Later my husband told me there were rumours of this predator showering young Filipino female office staff with jewellery, following sexual liaisons. I told my husband not to be so naïve. I said he probably sexually assaulted them and used the gifts to get away with it. However, it was during an outing with the Ladies Group, sitting in a canoe, in the middle of a lake, that I learnt just how experienced this monster was.

The Philippines is rich with natural beauty and near the end of my husband's contract the Ladies Group took a day trip to a beautiful lunch spot. After dining in the shallow peaceful flow of a river at the bottom of a waterfall, we went canoeing on the lake. My canoe buddy told me she wished she'd spent more time with me. When I asked her why she hadn't, she explained the predator's wife had told her group her husband didn't want her socialising with me because he had a more senior position than my husband. I told her the real reason was probably the attempted rape. As I told her what had happened, I watched her go deathly quiet and pale. I knew what was coming. I know the signs. She shared with me his repeated sexual assaults of herself and other women.

Apparently, on group outings he'd squash up next to her in the backseat of a car, cross his arms and slide his hand across and fondle her breast. He'd slide his hand under her bottom and touch her genitals. He'd even reach forward and do this to her when she was sitting in the front seat next to her husband. She froze, shock set in, she felt powerless, and he continued to assault her. What empowerment for him to assault a woman right under her husband's nose.

I asked her why they hadn't told their husbands. She said she didn't know how to. Typical victim response garden variety predators rely on.

On returning to Australia in 2012, already experiencing perimenopause, my anxiety increased, and for some time, I incorrectly explained it as menopause related. However, when it got to the point where I wanted to take a knife to bed for protection and my hypervigilance was running rampant, I knew it was more than menopause. I knew I was in trouble. I made a call to Susan Kendall. Susan explained heightened symptoms weren't unusual. She explained my returning to Australia as well as my children reaching ages where I'd been sexually assaulted would affect me. She recommended I get more counselling.

Having made an appointment to see a GP, sitting in the consultation room with a beautiful young female Indian doctor, I found myself confronted with the filth of what I'd lived through. In that moment I couldn't bring myself to contaminate this lovely young lady with that filth. When she asked what was wrong, I said, "I can't tell you." Misunderstanding my difficulty, she asked me to leave.

I got up and walked into the hallway. I stood there, rooted to the spot. I knew I needed help; I couldn't leave, I couldn't think straight and didn't know what to do next. A lovely staff member asked me if I was okay. I told her I wasn't. She found an empty office, and an older female doctor helped me through the anxiety attack, and we made a plan.

Initially, she referred me to a psychiatrist to whom I made it clear medication was not an option. I knew what I needed, and she recommended psychologist visits. The NSW Sexual Assault Tribunal gave me Dr Darina Rich's details. As discussed, Dr Rich is a very experienced no-nonsense sexual assault counsellor. Through working with her, I was able to once again take control of my symptoms and move ahead, adding to my skill set.

This concludes my story, from my perspective, told to the best of my ability. Thank you for your courage in taking this journey with me. I hope it has given you a way forward. An insight into sexual assault. An understanding and appreciation of the trauma sexual assault Victims are faced with, the devastation it has on Victims' lives and a realisation of the need to stamp out the current sexual assault epidemic.

Please have a plan. Practise the language you will need to use if you must call for help. Never blame yourself or anyone else for being a Victim, it's always the predator's fault. Remember if others react unhelpfully, they might not know what to do or they may be struggling with their own beliefs. Regardless that's their problem. Message to self could be only listen to what is helpful.

If you're a Victim, please tell yourself "Its not my fault" and get support.

COURT—
DO IT FOR YOU

In my experience innocent until proven guilty means the accused predator has all the power. However, I used the court process to transform into a Survivor.

It's not possible for every Victim to prosecute their abuser. NO judgement. Some are stuck in a Victim mindset and they're not ready, others find it too confronting. Alternatively, many Victims have told me the police won't charge citing: "He said she said." I hope this book wipes that thinking away for every reader. I've made the difference between rape and sex clear; it comes down to consent!

Go to another police station and tell them, "I didn't consent."

However, I advocate it's empowering to hold the sexual predator/s legally accountable despite the outcome. It helps Victims transform into Survivors. Further, the more Victims come forward, report to police and give a statement the greater public awareness becomes, allowing society to understand the epidemic proportions of sexual assault and the damage it does.

Prior to court I made two police statements, which were filed on record. I was told he did not. This shocked me. He entered court with no established position.

In 1996, standing on the steps of the Paramatta Criminal Court, with another of his Victims, I was told Mr Pleaded Guilty was pleading guilty to my police statement. I was told sexual predators don't plead guilty unless it's in their best interest. His other Victim was upset. She'd come to see him held accountable, get what he deserved. I explained to her, his pleading guilty to assaulting me was an acknowledgement of her pain and mine. I told her his pleading guilty meant more than a jury finding him guilty. Together we cried.

For me, the importance of having him charged and prosecuted wasn't to seek revenge. It wasn't to make him pay. That would have been a fool's erand. For me, this process allowed me to say what he did was wrong, it wasn't my fault, and to take back my personal power. This process helped me regain control over my life, and to become a Survivor.

I advocate the outcome isn't important. It should never be the focus. A Victim's focus should always be on themselves not the predator. Yes, it's difficult. However, it's important to approach law and order with a Survivor mindset rather than being trapped in a Victim mindset. Predators don't matter. In my experience, and that of others, holding the predator accountable, regardless of whether they're convicted or not, helps the Victim.

Never allow a jury's findings to matter. We need a jury system; however, accept it's flawed. A jury of our peers can be riddled with prejudice and ignorance.

The jury could include unidentified rapists and paedophiles. It could also include victims of sexual assault who are in denial. This denial could lead a juror to experience trauma from their own assault during a Victim's testimony. This could cause resentment toward the Victim.

You never know who is in a jury pool. Therefore, not guilty verdicts should have no meaning to a Victim.

Remember, people don't like to hear about incest or rape. Juries are made up of people who might not want to believe that someone could do such a thing. They might not want to be there. They might be uncomfortable with being responsible for sending someone to jail. Easier to believe the victim was mistaken or lying. You can't allow other people's judgements to rob you of your transformation into a Survivor.

Throughout my life the truth was my greatest strength. Anyone who experiences sexual assault should hold on to the truth, because it's the only honest thing you will ever find in your life. You don't need 12 people to tell you what happened, you lived through it. You know what happened, and nothing can change that. So be brave, be bold and do it for wonderful, special YOU, or support someone you care about to reclaim their identity.

If you go through the court system with any other agenda than meeting your social responsibilities and to aid your transformation to be a Survivor, then you risk deeper damage.

My Experience ...

Prior to court I remember my Department of Public Prosecutions (DPP) solicitor, asking me what sentence I wanted Mr Pleaded Guilty to get. I told him that wasn't my responsibility.

I had three responsibilities ...

- I'm legally required to report him for committing a crime
- Morally I reported him to protect others becoming his victims
- Most importantly, my responsibility to myself to become a Survivor.

Reporting him was part of my Survivor process. The self-respect that comes from the courage of holding a predator accountable was enough for me.

I had one thing that can never be taken from me or any sexual assault Victim/Survivor, the Truth. I knew it didn't matter what a jury believed. It didn't matter what the judge chose as punishment, it would never be enough. It only mattered that I stood up for myself and said, "You sexually assaulted me, it's wrong and I'm holding you accountable." I went to court for me.

I knew holding on to revenge was the road to disappointment and being trapped in Victim mode again. If that happened, he'd continue to hurt me. Please focus on you. Use the court process to empower yourself. Use it to take back what he/she/they took from you. Stand up, be proud of yourself for doing so, and say, "I didn't consent, you sexually assaulted me, it's wrong and I'm holding you accountable."

I found throughout the court process the focus is on protecting the predator. The Victim is on trial. The policeman shadowing my case judged my motivation and questioned why I was entering my Victim Impact Statement. During the sentencing trial, I remember Mr Pleaded Guilty's lawyer accused me of taking him to court because I was angry with him. Yes, of course I was angry, he'd raped me! Holding him legally accountable and filing my Victim Impact Statement was to help me, it had nothing to do with Mr Pleaded Guilty. However, a victim's motivation should never be on trial.

In my experience, within the court process there are two parties, the prosecution and the defence, and for me, three stages:

Stage One:

The preliminary process included Mr Pleaded Guilty entering a plea. During this stage his rights were absolute. He used the system to delay entering his plea, to draw out the process.

The delays and waiting were upsetting and exhausting for me. I remember being so disappointed each time there was a delay in entering a plea. I felt as though my life was in limbo, with the rape foremost in my mind. I worked hard during this time to find distractions, including a lot of swimming with my girlfriend. The Royal North Shore Sexual Assault Unit supported me every step of the way, and their resourceful advice was invaluable. I do think the length of time between delays was far too long, thoughtless and disrespectful to me, the Victim.

I had a simple sentence I would say to myself with each delay: "Every piece of sh*t gets his day and you're just another step closer to yours!" I was in for the long haul. If you decide to go to court, make sure you have the support to get you there.

Apparently, using delays is a typical tactic the defence team rely on. It weakens their opponent, the Victim. Sadly, I was told this defence tactic has led to Victims withdrawing their complaints.

During this process, I met with my DPP solicitor to talk about what to expect on the stand. He told me not to get upset. I think he regretted giving me that advice. I told him, "I'm a human being who's been raped, not a robot. I'm upset and I'm not going to lie about it."

In my opinion, forcing the Victim to bury their feelings at an extremely vulnerable time is totally unacceptable and destructive to the Victim. Further this practice doesn't allow for the whole truth. Trauma goes hand in hand with sexual assault.

Apparently, juries don't like victims getting upset. Juries should get upset that one human being/human beings could do so much damage to another human being. As a juror I'd expect to see the signs of sexual assault trauma when the Victim testifies; sadly, I know it's shunned upon.

Victims I've spoken to have told me that it was implied to them if they get upset on the stand, it's their fault if the jury goes against them. WOW, in my opinion, that's a damaging, manipulative guilt trip and totally unacceptable.

However, prejudice surrounding emotions isn't restricted to juries. I've been in a courtroom where a judge punished a Victim for being human. At a preliminary hearing, to establish if an ex-partner sexual assault case could proceed to trial, the case was dismissed because the Victim was crying. The judge said she felt it would be too traumatic for the Victim to cope with a trial. The Victim had made a commitment to herself. She was sitting there answering questions clearly and thoroughly. In my opinion, how dare any judge do this? Why destroy the Victim again?

At the time the judge's behaviour struck me as the most cowardly act I'd ever seen, alongside the Victim's incredible bravery. Personally, it continues to disgust me whenever I think of it.

Stage Two:

In my experience, if you're lucky enough to make it to trial, then you, the Victim, are on trial. It's so hard for Victims to get to court, and then the system carves them up. I've observed defence attorneys control the dialogue and, in my opinion, this needs to change. Mr Pleaded Guilty pled guilty.

I went on trial at sentencing, to prove the level of suffering in my Victim Impact Statement was true. I was told this was a precendent case, so I had no expectation of receiving the conduct protection currently afforded victims. I was told a top prosecution Silk flew from Perth to discredit my impact statement. I walked into Liverpool Court prepared for any outcome. I knew the truth, that's all that mattered.

If you make it to court, hugs and congratulations, you're very brave. Work with your counsellor and Survivor coach. Prepare yourself for the possibility of the jury finding the predator not guilty. This is important. I did this with my lovely group and counsellors. You know the predator is guilty and your focus must be on celebrating your strength to stand up against the monster in an environment I consider stacked against the Victim. Irrespective of the verdict, throw a party to celebrate YOU, because you won, you held him/her/them accountable. That took courage; acknowledge it!

Stage Three:

Sentencing. Prior to sentencing is when I entered my Victim Impact Statement. Victims, be brave, be honest, tell it all.

In 1997, while holidaying in Perth with my friend, I was given a choice. I could choose to leave my Victim Impact Statement on record for sentencing and the judge would grant the defence access to all my counselling notes. Alternatively, I could remove my Victim Impact Statement and keep my pain and suffering silent. For the first time in my life, I was determined to put myself first. Becoming a Survivor motivated me to live through two days of hell, so I could take back my personal power and my identity. I put myself on the line and trusted in the truth, for my benefit, regardless of the outcome. When I told Susan Kendall to give them my records, she told me she knew I would say that. She had them ready. The defence knew I'd leave my statement with the court and were waiting for my notes.

My Victim Impact Statement was my voice in a court system where the Victim doesn't count. In 1997, I went to court, and despite his guilty plea relived all the rapes. The truth held out.

The only time within the three litigation stages I counted, when my voice was heard, and my trauma considered was through my Victim

Impact Statement. I recommend every victim file an Impact Statement because you need to count!

I had a dinner to celebrate my Victim Impact Statement being accepted. For me it was a humbling experience.

Holding Mr Pleaded Guilty accountable for the impact he had on me was a huge achievement and it helped me make enormous strides towards the Survivor I am today.

Given the serious impact the rape had on me, Mr Pleaded Guilty was sentenced to weekend jail for twelve months.

A CALL TO ACTION

I t's never too late to transform.

If nobody you tell believes you, don't stop looking for support. There are great people out there who can really help you become a Survivor.

So, if the jury finds the predator not guilty does that mean you're a liar? No! Nothing will change what has happened to you. You know the truth, that's all that matters. Use the court experience to transform.

So, you're scared, should that stop you? No! Of course, you're going to be scared, but act. Action is empowering. Be proud when you speak out.

So, your friends and/or family aren't helpful; that's okay, find a sexual assault counsellor and Survivor coach. They'll help you.

Yes, it's hard, but transformation has its rewards. It's harder to remain a Victim.

So, you don't want anyone to know. That's Victim thinking and will hurt you. What happened to you wasn't your fault. You have nothing to be ashamed of and the rest of your life to look forward to. Focus on caring for you and building a life you're passionate about.

So, it was your father, uncle, aunt, grandmother, grandfather. It makes no difference who hurt you, they hurt you, and they shouldn't have!

So, they say you deserved it! So what? After reading *Insight* you know you didn't. You don't need other people to tell you what you know. If you listen to people, make sure they are qualified to give you an opinion.

So, your family are angry with you. Probably not the first time, probably won't be the last. Remember, if they can't cope, that's not your problem. You can't change them. They can sort themselves out. Your responsibility is to yourself. Focus on you. Become a Survivor.

So, it was a long time ago. Doesn't matter, find an excellent counsellor and/or Survivor coach, become a Survivor.

So, as a Victim you've done dumb things. Who hasn't! Don't judge, get focused on the rest of your life. The part where you're the Survivor!

So, you feel embarrassed; that's the Victim talking not the Survivor. Get a counsellor, get a coach, become a Survivor.

So, this counsellor isn't helping. Find another one. Find a Survivor coach. Become a Survivor. You might try several counsellors before you find one that helps you.

So, you feel alone; you're not! There are thousands of people just like you. Find a counsellor, get a Survivor coach, join a group and become a Survivor!

So, you cry; that's good, cry. Tears led me to becoming a Survivor.

So, you think no-one will believe you. Not true, find a good support group, a counsellor, a coach and find out for yourself, lots of people will believe you.

So, it's not your fault. Don't wallow in self-pity, get moving, you've got work to do to become a Survivor.

Act or stay dead! The choice is up to you!

AFTERWORD

Our Insight journey into the profile of sexual assault has come to an end. Congratulations.

If you're interested in finding out more about Insight and the work I do, check me out at michelleinsight.com.au

Remember, be Aware, be Prepared, take Care of yourself and become a Survivor!

STAY UPDATED

Come visit Insight for your dose of inspiration and up-to-date content at www.michelleinsight.com.au

ANY QUESTIONS?

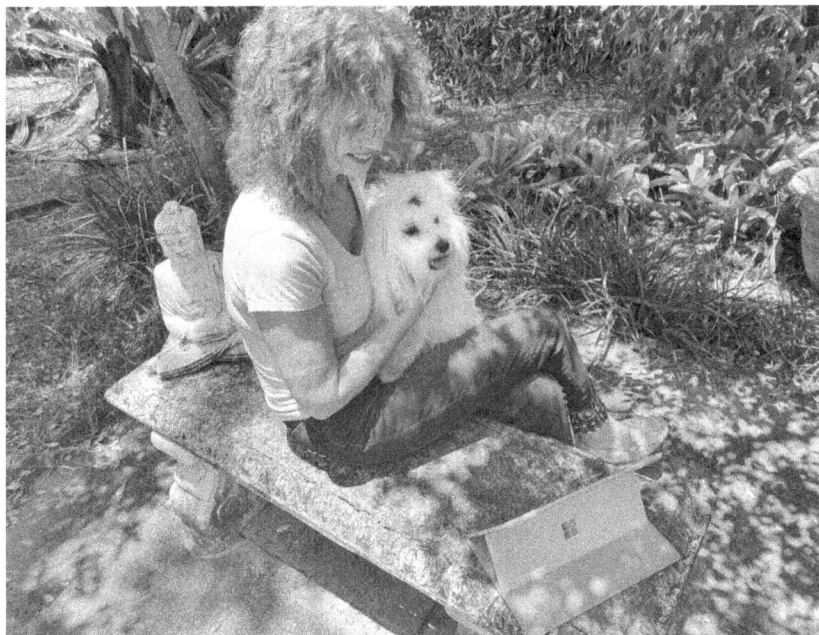

For your chance to have a 20-minute consultation with the author email info@michelleinsight.com.au

INSPIRATION AND ENLIGHTENMENT

To enquire about Michelle speaking at your group, club or event email her at info@michelleinsight.com.au for availability and bookings.

If her schedule permits Michelle will speak for free at not-for-profit organisations.

RESOURCE
BIBLIOGRAPHY

Aphrodite Matsakis, P. (2003). *The Rape Recovery Handbook*. Oakland, CA 94609: New Harbinger Publications, Inc.

Atkinson, M. (2010). *Resurection after rape: A guide to transforming from victum to survivior* (2nd ed.). Oklahoma: RAR Publishing.

Gallagher, R. (2014). *From Surviving to Thriving Recovery for Survivors of Abuse*. San Bernardino: Createspace Independent Publishing Platform.

Gavey, N. (2019). *Just Sex? The Cultural Scaffolding Of Rape* (2nd ed.). New York: Routledge.

Girolamo, E. d. (2003, October 20). *I was 14 when I was gang raped*. Retrieved from The Guardian: https://www.theguardian.com/world/2003/oct/20/gender.biography

Harding, K. (2015). *Asking for It The Alrming Rise of Rape Culture - and What We Can Do About It*. Boston: Da Capo Press.

Harvard Health Publishing. (n.d.). *Understanding the stress response.* Retrieved December 1, 2019, from https://www.health.harvard.edu/ staying-healthy/understanding-the-stress-response

Kitching, C. (2019). *Paedophiles are born - not made - and nothing can change them, study finds.* Retrieved from Mirror: https://www.mirror.co.uk/ news/world-news/paedophiles-born-not-made-nothing-20803970

Ladylike. (2019). *Devin Shares Her Sexual Assault Story.* Retrieved from Youtube: https://www.youtube.com/watch?v=Es2lmv_wJnY

Michelle Stevens, P. (2017). *Scared Selfless My Journey from Abuse and Madness to Surviving and Thriving.* New York: G. P. Putnam's Sons.

Phillips, J., & Park, M. (2006). *Measuring domestic violence and sexual assault against women.* Retrieved 2019, from Parliament of Australia: https://www.aph.gov.au/about_parliament/parliamentary_ departments/parliamentary_library/publications_archive/archive/ violenceagainstwomen

RAINN (Rape, Abuse & Incest National Network). (2019, December 1). *Effects of Sexual Violence.* Retrieved from Rainn.org: https://www. rainn.org/effects-sexual-violence

RAINN (Rape, Abuse & Incest National Network). (2019). *What Consent Looks Like.* Retrieved from Rainn.org: https://www.rainn. org/articles/what-is-consent

Reachout Australia. (2019). *5 things you need to know about sexual consent.* Retrieved from reachout.com: https://au.reachout.com/ articles/5-things-you-need-to-know-about-sexual-consent

Reachout Austrlaia. (2019). *5 things you need to know about sexual consent.* Retrieved from Reachout.com: https://au.reachout.com/ articles/5-things-you-need-to-know-about-sexual-consent

Remarkable, P. (2013). *Positivley Remarkable People*. Retrieved from Susan kendall am, social worker and international mentor: https://positivelyremarkable.wordpress.com/2013/12/03/susan-kendall/

Saskatoon Sexual Assault and Information Centre (SSAIC). (2019). *Triggers: What Are They?* Retrieved from Saskatoon Sexual Assault and Information Centre (SSAIC): https://ssaic.ca/learn/triggers-what-are-they/

Sexual Assault Prevention and Awareness Center (SAPAC). (2018, January). *Understanding the Perpertrator.* Retrieved from Sexual Assault Prevention and Awareness Center: https://sapac.umich.edu/article/understanding-perpetrator

Teenager who was sexually assaulted multiple times ends her own life after requesting legal euthanasia. (2019, 06 04). Retrieved from Independant: https://www.independent.co.uk/news/world/europe/euthanasia-clinic-suicide-depression-rape-anorexia-netherlands-teenager-noa-pothoven-a8944356.html

The Daniel Morcombe Foundation. (2019). *The Daniel Morcombe Foundation.* Retrieved from The Daniel Morcombe Foundation: https://danielmorcombefoundation.com.au/

Victorian Centres Against Sexual Assault (CASA) Forum. (2019). *Fact Sheet: Statistics About Sexual Assault.* Retrieved from Centres Against Sexual Assualt (CASA): http://www.casa.org.au/casa_pdf.php?document=statistics

Wikipedia. (2018, July). *Causes of sexual violence.* Retrieved from Wikipedia: https://en.wikipedia.org/wiki/Causes_of_sexual_violence

NOTES